info@9marks.org | www.9marks.org

Tools like this are provided by the generous investment of donors.
Each gift to 9Marks helps equip church leaders with a biblical vision and practical resources for displaying God's glory to the nations through healthy churches.

Donate at: www.9marks.org/donate.

Or make checks payable to "9Marks" and mail to:
9 Marks
525 A St. NE
Washington, DC 20002

Editorial Director: Jonathan Leeman
Editor: Sam Emadi
Managing Editor: Alex Duke
Layout: Rubner Durais
Cover Design: OpenBox9
Production Manager: Rick Denham & Mary Beth Freeman
9Marks President: Mark Dever
Paperback: 978-1-958168-47-9
eBook: 978-1-958168-48-6

Editor's Note:

CHURCH ADMINISTRATION

Jonathan Leeman

Church administration is not my favorite church topic. Probably not top twenty, in fact. Yet when you need it, you need it.

Who should you hire? When should you fire? How much should you pay? What job titles should you use? What about pastoral sabbaticals and retirement contributions? What's a constitution good for? These might not be soul-energizing questions but answering them well is a mandate of love for the church.

I learned as a young husband that, while I might want to celebrate "spontaneity" or "taking it easy," loving my wife sometimes meant making plans, thinking ahead, establishing a few structures. This is what living with someone else, and not as a single man, means. So it is in a church. Working together well and peaceably requires attending to administration.

We asked a number of lead pastors and administration or executive pastors to help us think through matters like staffing, building, budgets and other policies. As I read every article, I found myself asking a host of further questions I would not have thought to ask before. I trust you'll discover the same. Even if we don't answer every question you have (far from it, I assume), you'll have a better sense of which questions to begin asking.

Paul left Titus in Crete to "put what remained into order" (Titus 1:5). He also told the Corinthians, "all things should be done decently and in order" (1 Cor. 14:40). He was talking about the church gathering, of course, but the lesson applies more broadly. Pastors and deacons build up the body of Christ by caring for the staffing structures, pay policies, and building budgets. We pray this Journal will help.

ABOUT THE AUTHOR

Jonathan (@JonathanLeeman) edits the 9Marks series of books as well as the 9Marks Journal. He is also the author of several books on the church. Since his call to ministry, Jonathan has earned a master of divinity from Southern Seminary and a Ph.D. in Ecclesiology from the University of Wales. He lives with his wife and four daughters in Cheverly, Maryland, where he is an elder at Cheverly Baptist Church.

Is Administration for Pastors?

THE NEW TESTAMENT'S FIRST ADMINISTRATORS

Brad Thayer

Pastoral ministry comes with many hardships, including administrative challenges. It's part of the calling to be "servants of Christ and stewards of the mysteries of God" (1 Cor. 4:1; cf. 2 Cor. 11:23–33).

I've had my fair share of admin challenges over the years. They've often come unannounced, demanding immediate attention. In 2008, the stock market plummeted the week I moved to Atlanta. Giving declined when the church was over a million dollars in debt. Most support staff resigned within three months of new pastoral leadership. I had to figure out the church's operations with a notebook of outdated instructions. At one point, the sewage backed up into the children's hall on a Sunday morning. And most painfully, in my tenth year, the financial assistant was caught embezzling thousands of dollars.

These types of challenges and countless others, big and small, can leave pastors discouraged. And this may be no fault of their own. Their church may have unrealistic expectations that they preach excellent sermons *and* oversee the facility. Some pastors become disgruntled because they have ministry misperception. They think ministry runs on two rails that never intersect—pastoral and admin. When the admin crosses the pastoral, they're frustrated because it interrupts the "real" ministry of teaching and discipling.

Administrative challenges are not new to pastors and churches. In the first century, the church in Jerusalem experienced botched administration during its infancy. And the apostles' solution to appoint servants (let's call them the New Testament's first "administrators") is instructive today. From Acts 6:1–7, I want to show how good administration is a priceless service to both a church's health and elders' leadership.

ACTS 6:1–7: THE NEW TESTAMENT'S FIRST ADMINISTRATORS

Throughout Acts, Luke summarizes how the gospel spread: "the Word of the Lord continued to increase" (Acts 19:20; cf. 6:7; 9:31; 12:24; 16:5; 28:30–31). But something always threatened the church. As soon as it was birthed in Jerusalem, corruption and persecution tested its commitment (Acts 5:1–42).

In Acts 6:1–7, the apostles faced a new challenge. They struggled to care for widows as "the disciples were increasing in number" (v. 1). And with limited time and energy, the apostles couldn't tend to benevolence *and* word ministry (vv. 2, 4). Both were important. But they were too much for one group. As a result of poor administrative oversight, disunity broke out among the members (v. 1). No longer were they of "one heart and soul" (Acts 4:32).

The apostles were also at a crossroads. They couldn't forsake their primary calling. They were commissioned to preach the gospel, not "serve tables" (v. 2). But caring for widows and restoring unity were critical to the church's health. Love and unity were at stake if "serving tables" wasn't given due administrative attention.

In God's providence, the apostles came up with a plan. They asked the church to pick out godly, wise men to administer the benevolence so they could devote themselves to "prayer and the ministry of the word" (vv. 3–4). The congregation saw the wisdom in this: "what they said *pleased* the whole gathering" (v. 5; emphasis added). They "chose" seven men and set them before the apostles to be commissioned to service (v. 6). The church kept word and mercy ministry in proper relationship.

The seven's administrative ministry was a significant undertaking. They were entrusted with restoring unity that was fractured along cultural lines between Hellenists and Hebraic believers. They needed wisdom for problem solving. Their solution couldn't run roughshod over the pain of a widow who was hurt from being neglected. The church was comprised of thousands of believers. It was a high cost if they didn't properly administer the daily distribution. A poor administrative solution would deepen the fissure. They were dealing in relational capital essential to a church's health—love and unity. So they had to be full of the Spirit.

Whatever means the seven used to meet the need, the Lord blessed it. Luke wrote, "The Word of God continued to increase, and the number of the disciples multiplied greatly in Jerusalem, and a great many of the priests became obedient to the faith" (v. 7). The administrative challenge of a growing church's benevolence ministry ultimately didn't distract from the gospel. The seven's service proved to be a priceless gift to the apostles' ministry and church's unity.

LESSONS FOR OVERSEEING ADMINISTRATIVE CHALLENGES

There will be administrative challenges when believers covenant to love and provide for the needs of one another. Instead of pastors begrudging these challenges, they should find ways to oversee and utilize members to meet them. Here are some ways they can do this:

1. Find qualified, gifted servants.

Acts 6 is as a good paradigm for separating the responsibilities of elders and deacons. Deacons are to safeguard the church's unity by meeting physical needs so elders can devote themselves to prayer and the ministry of the Word.

Pastors are often overwhelmed with admin demands because they've undervalued the office of deacon and members' gifts of service. They've taken on too much responsibility for physical needs that should be met by deacons and members. Qualified, gifted servants free a pastor of many burdens by ensuring members are cared for and ministries are coordinated.

It blesses pastors to have servants who eagerly keep Word ministry central. A servant's instinct should be to relieve the pastor of admin burdens and members' physical needs so he is well prepared to preach. They should ask, "What tasks might we do so Sunday School teachers have excellent lessons? How can we coordinate volunteers so children and youth teachers are ready to engage kids with the Word? Are the right people managing the finances so our elders are free to minister Scripture to members personally?" Finding qualified, gifted servants helps to ensure the Word remains central and physical needs are met.

2. Identify the pastoral implications of administration.

Not all admin responsibilities have pastoral implications. If the AC goes out, someone needs to get it fixed. But if it goes out and the church has to figure out alternative arrangements for gathering, a pastor or some elders should think through pastoral implications of those arrangements. The pastoral concern in Acts 6 was relational disunity caused by broken administration. The seven's solution had to aim to restore unity.

Pastors should care about their church's administrative operations. They should know them well enough to identify their pastoral implications. This is especially true of communication, finances, and facility renovations.

Take finances, for example. Treasurers and deacons can present helpful and informative financial reports at member's meetings. But are these reports about more than finances? I believe so. They're opportunities to set a pastoral tone and provide biblical instruction about giving and a church's priorities. So it's good to have an elder give the financial report and any pastoral implications.

3. Delegate with direction and encouragement.

Delegation entails the humble recognition that no pastor is omnicompetent. He needs others. And his church may be full of members with diverse gifts willing to help (1 Cor. 12:4–11). They support the elders' leadership and are happy to serve "wherever is needed." They just need a job with direction and encouragement.

It's a pastor's responsibility to explain why a ministry needs coordination. Why should members use their time and energy? What's the purpose of overseeing administrative tasks? If members understand the elders' vision for a ministry, they'll often happily employ their gifts to meet it. Their hands are strengthened to serve when given clear direction.

Members also need encouragement. I often tell support staff, "Your job is to equip *and resource* members for ministry in the church." Sometimes the best encouragement is to provide people the right tools for the job. An encouraging word from a pastor also goes a long way. Administration usually goes unseen and underappreciated. So a "thank you!" or "I praise God for your service!" will encourage their hearts.

CONCLUSION

Satan is cunning. He'll use any means necessary to threaten a church's commitment to preach the Word and maintain unity. His weapon of choice may even be a poor admin process to subvert a church's commitment. And yet, God's Spirit gives his church every sufficient gift for her good, including the priceless service of good administration.

ABOUT THE AUTHOR

Brad Thayer is an associate pastor/administration of Mount Vernon Baptist Church in Sandy Springs, Georgia.

Administrators

PLAYING WITH CALCULATORS OR BUILDING UP THE BODY OF CHRIST?

Mike Carnicella

Every year I go on a retreat with administrative pastors from like-minded churches. And every year, Alex Duke (9Marks editor and my coworker at church) makes fun of me. "What are you guys going to do? Pull out your TI83 calculators? Look at a bunch of spreadsheets together?" Ha ha ha.

Jokes aside, the average member of my church (and I'd assume other churches as well) does not have a good idea of what an administrative pastor *actually does*. Vague thoughts of building maintenance or paying the bills are usually what people have in mind. Sure, we often handle those things or supervise someone else who does. But being an administrative pastor is much more than that. At the end of the day, good administration is necessary for a healthy church.

WHAT'S ADMINISTRATION—AND WHO'S GOOD FOR IT?

What is administration? Likely, one of the first things we think about when we hear the word administration is government: "Under my administration…" or "This administration has done…." Has the church today co-opted this word? I don't think so.

The word can be translated a few different ways: administering, leadership, or even governing. In other words, it involves leading or guiding. The apostle Paul also lists administration as a spiritual gift (Rom. 12:8 and 1 Cor. 12:28). The Holy Spirit has equipped some people in the church in this way so that they might build up the body of Christ.

So how do you know if you are gifted for administration in the church?

I've seen many people from different backgrounds succeed in administration, but one common characteristic seems to be an ability to focus on details. Detail-oriented people often find their way into administrative roles. Sometimes this characteristic is indicative of someone being supernaturally gifted in administration. In this case, and like other gifts, administration can be nourished and improved. There are naturally gifted teachers and preachers, but even these people can improve their gifts and skills by practicing them and learning from others.

What kind of board game player are you? Do you like to jump in and learn as you go? Or do you want to open the manual, read the rules, and understand them before you play? I would guess that many administrative pastors belong to the latter group. We can call this the "board game rule of thumb." (Administrative pastors are also often very creative!) Often, church administration is not unlike playing a very complex board game. I'm not talking about Settlers of Catan. That's just a gateway board game. My eight-year-old can play that. I'm talking about Agricola, a real board game. Of course, leading a church in the area of administration is not a game. The people are real, and the stakes can be high. And how you administrate can either harm or help.

WHY GOOD ADMINISTRATION IS IMPORTANT

Administration is not only biblical; it's necessary. It might not be your thing, but it can't be ignored. *Someone* needs to know all the rules or policies and be able to administer them correctly. Without clear rules (a constitution and accompanying policies), a group of individuals is likely to fall into either tyranny or anarchy. The church is no different.

Therefore, I'd argue that an administrative person is one of the most critical positions a church can hire. As a lead pastor in a small but growing church, you're often faced with the question of whom to hire first. Should you hire someone to help with worship gatherings? Should you hire someone to handle missions or discipleship? It depends somewhat on the skillset of each lead pastor, but I would argue that the first hire generally should be someone who can help in administration. This is especially true if the lead pastor is not gifted in administration.

Of course, administration and policies cannot simply be taken from one church and plugged into another. Administrative structures and policies vary from church to church. This is because policies are regularly created in the wake of a problem to prevent the problem from coming up again. Regardless of having first-hand experience with a problem or not, policies for things like handling money, child safety, and appointing leaders are necessary. Introducing a new policy is a wisdom issue. Hopefully, you'll have a plurality of elders to help you make these decisions, but it often falls to those in administration to lead the way.

What does someone involved in administration actually do? Everything from handling finances to building upkeep and renovations to the oft-overlooked development of various church-related policies. These three tasks may seem tedious, but they're extremely valuable to a healthy, happy church.

You may not be able to find chapter and verse to demonstrate their importance, but even the early church found similar issues popping up. For example, Acts 6 features an administration issue. There was a dispute in the church, and with it came potential division and distraction. The Greek-speaking Christians felt neglected relative to the Hebrew-speaking Christians. The apostles stepped in to create a new team of servants to address this issue. Many believe they were the first deacons. These servants helped to preserve the church's unity by way of their administration.

It's no different in our churches today. Sometimes unforeseen problems arise, and we must react. Problem-solving is at the heart of good administration. In my experience, being trained as an engineer has often proved helpful in church administration because engineering school is basically four years of problem-solving. Seeing problems in advance and creating systems or policies to avoid them is a big part of my job. Reacting to problems and figuring out how to solve them is just as important.

I would wager that many churches learned valuable administration and problem-solving lessons over the last couple of years. I doubt that many churches had pandemic policies in place before 2020. Did your church create any new policies during the pandemic? We can debate the merits of having a livestream and whom you should allow to watch it if it's not public. But how many churches started a livestream during the pandemic and now can't figure out how to turn it off or at least limit who has access to it? Without a policy for its use, there will always be a tendency toward what's easiest. Once the livestream has been started, it's easy to just keep it going because turning it off will require hard conversations. "Are you saying that you *don't* want people to hear the gospel? That's unloving. That's limiting your reach." Maybe. Or maybe you need to have a challenging conversation with someone, so they will start coming back to church, where people gather in person. This is just one example of what it looks like to think through a problem and come to a solution that seeks to love and protect the flock.

Good administration and good administrators are a gift from God. Don't neglect these gifts just because they seem boring or nerdy. That may be true, but God has given these gifts to build up and protect the unity of the church.

ABOUT THE AUTHOR

Mike Carnicella is an associate pastor for administration of Third Avenue Baptist Church in Louisville, Kentucky.

Pastors, Don't Forget to Shepherd Your Deacons

Gus Pritchard

There's something good and right about a pastor fighting to stay out of the weeds of church administration. To put a slight spin on the apostles' words, "It is not right that we should give up preaching the Word of God to manage spreadsheets and review facility-use policies" (see Acts 6:2).

Nonetheless, there is a ditch on the other side to avoid, too. While we shouldn't focus too much on administration, we shouldn't totally ignore it.

God calls us to provide oversight to the entire ministry of our churches—including shepherding the deacons in their work.

TWO BIBLICAL PRINCIPLES

1. Elder oversight involves giving some attention to administration.

Several times the elders are said to exercise "oversight" or are simply called "overseers" (e.g. Acts 20:28; Phil. 1:1; 1 Tim. 3:1-2; Tit. 1:7; 1 Peter 5:3). The term suggests that their work includes superintending the entire local church. Walter Bauer's English-Greek lexicon explains how this word is closely related to the work of "one who has the responsibility of safeguarding," "a supervisor, with special interest in guarding the apostolic tradition." The Louw-Nida lexicon states that the word "overseer" captures both "the responsibility of caring for the needs of a congregation as well as directing the activities of the membership." This suggests the elders' work includes a level of administrative authority.

Consider also the example of the apostles in Acts 6:1–7, who functioned in a pastor-like way. They provide guidance to the entire church for solving the food distribution problem. They didn't merely inform the church of their duties, and then walk away. They offered a concrete solution: appoint proto-deacons.

Paul also gave a detailed set of instructions to Timothy, who functioned as a pastor, about his church's benevolence ministry. And to some extent he gets into the nitty-gritty: support widows who meet these particular qualifications. In other words, Timothy should give some level of oversight to the physical care of widows in his pastoral role, even if a deacon gives more direct attention (1 Tim. 5:3ff).

In these kinds of examples, the New Testament suggests that a pastor's job includes some measure of administrative focus. While pastors give their chief attention to the state of the vine, doing so requires them to step back sometimes and inspect the condition of the trellis as well.

In other words, directing the affairs of the church means elder oversight extends even to the realm of deacons' work.

2. Elders ought to provide some degree of oversight to deacons' work.

The fact that the elders need to give broad oversight to the administration of the church means they give broad oversight to the work of the deacons.

Consider Acts 6 once more. We have no reason to think they managed the proto- deacons as they went about distributing food to widows, but they did specify who could serve in this capacity and put them in charge: "select from among you seven men of good reputation, full of the Spirit and wisdom, whom we will put in charge of this need" (Acts 6:3).

In general, commentators distinguish the spiritual concerns of the pastors (like sermons, Sunday school lessons, prayer meetings, and baptisms) from the tangible concerns of the deacons (like the building, the grounds, the security, and the finances), as in Matt Smethurst's book *Deacons.* And that's broadly accurate. At the same time, human beings are both physical and spiritual, and the two aspects of our persons are profoundly integrated. A church's overall ministry, therefore, should not try to wholly separate them either.

For instance, imagine the deacon of budget trying unilaterally to reduce missionary funding to pay for a major building project. The pastors, in response, might take issue!

In short, the Lord places both the spiritual and the tangible, to varying extents, under the oversight of the pastors. The extent of elder involvement over the work of deacons will vary, depending on how closely the deacon's work relates to the ministry of the word and the spiritual heath of the church.

BEST PRACTICES FOR LEADING DEACONS

Here are three pieces of advice on how pastors can give oversight to the administration of the church without getting swamped with spreadsheets and file folders.

1. Put elders in charge of the annual budget process.

Few matters of administration have more influence on the direction and shape of ministry than the church budget. What gets funded will eventually influence the overall direction of the church. For this reason, it's wise to put elders in charge of the annual budget process.

In our church, I serve as the pastor who gives oversight to the annual budget process. We have an incredibly capable deacon of budget, who does the vast majority of the number-crunching, the forecasting, and the coordinating of various data inputs. One of my main tasks includes setting and managing a budget-planning schedule. By doing this, I can ensure that the elders get enough time to scrutinize the budget before our members see it and vote on it.

The pastors' oversight of the annual budget process might look different at another church. It is generally good to keep pastors from getting lost in weeds of financial details. But it would also be unwise to not give the elders sufficient time to study and broadly shape the church's budget.

2. Find deacons who know when to defer to elders.

A good deacon must be capable of getting vital administrative tasks done with little supervision. Their work should be measured in part by how they protect the pastors and elders from distraction. And yet, a good deacon will also be comfortable with deferring big decisions to the pastors and elders. This instinct for deferral preserves the elders' oversight over the entire ministry of the church.

3. Build strong lines of communication between the deacons and elders.

Communication between the elders and deacons should be regular. After elder meetings, for instance, the elders should make sure they contact any deacons who might be affected by decisions the elders made. You don't want a deacon finding out about an elder decision that dramatically impacts their area of service at a members' meeting along with the rest of the congregation. That risks causing the deacons to feel like their work doesn't matter.

Likewise, deacons should be quick to report anything they do or see they think the elders might want to know. One thing to help facilitate this is to invite a deacon to every elder meeting and ask them if they have any updates or if there are ways the elders can better help the deacon.

CONCLUSION

In God's wisdom, he has given the church two offices: elders and deacons. They shouldn't function as two separate bodies of authority. Instead, God calls pastors and elders to lead the flock under their care, such that the work of the deacons causes the elder-led word ministry to flourish.

May this be true of all the places where Christ is faithfully preached!

ABOUT THE AUTHOR

Gus Pritchard is an associate pastor for Castleview Church in Indianapolis, Indiana.

From the Archives

WHY AN ADMINISTRATIVE PASTOR

Ryan Townsend

At 9Marks, one of our favorite books on pastoral ministry is Colin Marshall and Tony Payne's *The Trellis and the Vine*. The main idea is simple: in the disciple-making work of Christian ministry, the real growth that churches should pursue is the growth of the vine (Christians). Growing the church's trellises (administrative structures) is important only insofar as it helps the vine to grow.

If Marshall and Payne are correct, and we think they are, there are some clear implications for what kinds of staff a church should look to hire. For instance, a church may benefit from hiring a trellis-building administrative pastor.

Indeed, this is not the right course of action for all situations. However, I'd like to raise a few of the advantages of an administrative pastor for your consideration.

YOUR FIRST HIRE: A FAITHFUL PREACHER

The most important thing is to find a man gifted by God to preach the Bible. This is because God always saves and sanctifies through his Word. Like the apostle Paul, we must be willing to let everything else fail, if necessary, to continue preaching the gospel (e.g., Acts 20:18-24).

This means that if a church can only hire one pastor, it should be a man who can preach God's Word.

YOUR SECOND, THIRD, OR FOURTH HIRE: CONSIDER AN ADMINISTRATIVE PASTOR

Vine growth in a church is easier and more efficient with good "trellises"—strategy, structures, processes, tools, and communication. Trellises like these help us steward our resources and relationships and promote supernatural, gospel growth.

I was converted thirteen years ago at Capitol Hill Baptist Church. Since then, I've seen the immense value of Matt Schmucker's trellis work in our church. Now I get to work with Jamie Dunlop, the current executive pastor, who serves our church so well. I've also served as the administrative pastor at Clifton Baptist Church. From that chair, I experienced the pastoral demands and managed many details of our life together.

Often, preaching pastors make their second hire a general-duty associate pastor. The idea is that this man will help with teaching, counseling, worship, adult education, and children and family ministries. That makes sense. After all, a pastor needs backup in all these areas. But what about administration? Churches often fail to consider this a pastoral priority. I think this oversight can hinder the vine's growth. A man who is both a pastor and an administrator understands vine growth and stewards the trellises appropriately.

This brings us to why I think an administrative pastor is often a good hire. Remember, I am recommending a man who is qualified to pastor and who is a proficient administrator. A pastor because, well, the job is pastoral! He handles the big-picture (e.g., strategy and organization) and the small details (e.g., budget line items and members' meeting agendas). He must have sound theology, pastoral discernment, communication skills, preaching and teaching abilities, servant-hearted leadership, humility, love, and diplomacy in both fields. He also needs to be gifted in administration, organizational strategy, and communications because his job requires him to define, build, and manage the organization and its infrastructures. He must manage the church's strategy, processes, tools, and people.

NINE MORE REASONS TO HIRE AN ADMINISTRATIVE PASTOR

Here are nine more reasons why your church might benefit from hiring an administrative pastor:

1. Strategy

The preaching pastor will naturally influence and even drive the vision and voice of the church. But every vision requires someone to administrate and advance it in the area of its nuts and bolts. This takes time, patience, biblical knowledge, pastoral discernment, and hard work. A good administrative pastor brings these things to the table.

You might have seen the Charles Spurgeon portrait with a couple of men hidden in the shadowy background. Did you notice these men? This portrait reminds us that Spurgeon's ministry depended partly on brothers serving the church in the background. Most, if not all, good churches and pastors have such people.

2. Organization and Infrastructure

Typically, strategy consultants say that an organization will only succeed to the extent that clear processes and tools are in place to build, support, and maintain it. Gospel ministry is different because actual growth depends on God's aid. Still, churches must consider how to steward their resources faithfully through good trellises. And this is the job of the administrative pastor. He builds and maintains processes and tools for all the parts and pieces of the church. These nuts and bolts may include:

- managing building(s) and property
- overseeing the logistics, schedule, and events
- managing tasks, personalities, details for staff, membership processes, money, important church documents, etc.

3. Communication

The best plans and processes will fail if good communication and teaching are absent. Much of the responsibility for communication falls to the preaching pastor and elders as a whole. Still, the administrative pastor is a kind of glue that holds the staff, leadership, and members together. A good administrative pastor is 20/20 when it comes to details. At the same time, he aims to manage those details for the glory of God. Practically, this plays out in how he communicates to the church. He works so that all the parties hear and understand one another.

4. Member Care

Administrative pastors should look out for the congregation's needs that others may be unaware of. With pastoral discernment, love, and empathy, he will be able to act on behalf of the church so that they are faithful to care for one another. For example, he may help build an effective deacon team to serve the church's needs.

5. Staff Care

A good administrative pastor practically cares for the staff. He is the guy managing things like health care, compensation, housing, and the office culture. Further, he is a liaison between the church staff and other leaders. A good administrative pastor understands that businesses are profit-driven, and churches are relationship-driven. Managing these relationships is his business!

6. Stewardship and Finances

Church budgets and finances require pastoral qualification and discernment. The administrative pastor should be organized, efficient, above reproach, and trustworthy. He must manage and steward the church's resources faithfully. This work may include his appointing a competent, like-minded treasurer.

7. Teaching and Discipling

An administrative pastor should have the gift of teaching. This is a biblical requirement for all elders (1 Tim. 3:2)! Therefore, he should assist in the local church's regular teaching, discipling, and mentoring. Going above and beyond may also mean training and mentoring other men who aspire to a similar position.

8. Corporate Witness

Our God is a God of order, detail, and beauty. While a church's physical appearance should not sum up our growth strategy, it may subtly help or hinder its witness. A good administrative pastor should manage signage, landscaping, and the facilities for regular use by the church. This includes ensuring the grounds and building are safe for members and guests. His attention to detail may not be known, but it will undoubtedly be felt.

9. Glory of God

In many ways, the work of a good administrative pastor should go unnoticed. If he's doing his job well (with God's blessing), the church will run smoothly with him standing somewhat in the background. This doesn't mean that his work is unimportant. The administrative pastor's faithfulness supports the platform on which the preached Word goes forward. In so doing, he brings glory to God.

In short, the teaching and ministries of a healthy church can be wonderfully enabled and enhanced by faithful management, stewardship, and administration.

ABOUT THE AUTHOR

Ryan Townsend is the Executive Director of 9Marks, and an elder at Capitol Hill Baptist Church in Washington, D. C.

Staffing

HIRING AND FIRING

Brad Wheeler

You may not love it. In fact, you may be pretty bad at it, but you're still expected to do it. Seminaries don't teach it (in my experience), but your church's health depends on it. And more personally, your own longevity in ministry will often rise or fall because of it.

I'm talking about managing a church staff. I'm not so much referring to the *culture* of a church staff, though that's certainly critical. I'm referring more to the scaffolding, the authority structures, the supervisory and subordinate relationships. This subject doesn't excite me at all. But if managed poorly, it can make your life, your experience of ministry, and the ministry experience of those under you miserable.

So if you're the lead pastor (or an elder given charge of staff oversight), here are a few hard and humbling lessons I've learned along the way. And please keep in mind: much of what I'll share is more *prudential* than biblically *prescribed.*

1. CLEARLY DISTINGUISH BETWEEN ELDER AND NON-ELDER STAFF POSITIONS.

Most polity structures recognize this difference in some fashion. I pastor a congregational church, so the *congregation* has the formal authority to call *pastors* (lead pastor, associate pastors, assistant pastor, i.e. whoever is a pastor). The hiring of pastoral staff (e.g. pastoral assistants) and administrative staff is delegated to other staff elders. Ensure such matters are clearly delineated in your church bylaws or constitution, however your church is structured.

A word of encouragement: as much as possible, align your titles with biblical offices. So if the man is a pastor/elder, make that clear in his title (lead *pastor*, associate *pastor*, assistant *pastor*). It will be a regular reminder to all that he holds the biblical office of elder. If the individual is not in the formal office of pastor/elder, don't call him a pastor. He can be a pastoral assistant ("assistant" is his role, "pastoral" adjectivally describes what he does). Or he can have some other title, like "director."

Personally, I would avoid vague terms like "minister" as much as possible. Is the person an elder or not? Do they exercise pastoral authority, or are they merely servants (which is closer to the meaning of the word minister)? Avoid titles that obscure instead of clarify.

2. CLEARLY DELINEATE LINES OF AUTHORITY.

On smaller teams, detailed organizational charts aren't necessary. But the larger the team, the more important they become. When a staff member has a question about their job, role, expectations, performance, etc., it will serve them if they know who to go to.

Pastoral work can never be perfectly captured on a spreadsheet. And some individuals may work with multiple staff pastors. But seek to avoid a patchwork structure where someone feels as if they have two or three different bosses. That only creates confusion and frustration.

And lead pastor, avoid the temptation to overly insert yourself into conversations and decisions you've delegated to others. If you've handed authority to them, trust them. If you consistently don't trust them, then hire someone you do. But don't say you trust them and then second-guess them at every turn. That's a wonderful way to discourage them, and it will eventually lead to everything landing on your desk. And, as I've sadly learned, that serves nobody well.

3. CLEARLY COMMUNICATE EXPECTATIONS.

Pastoral ministry is all-encompassing work. And any valuable staff member will be willing to pitch in and serve wherever there's need.

That said, a job description is a useful tool in establishing expectations. Individuals should not be confused about what the church has set them apart to do. A clear job description helps them prioritize tasks and allocate time. It keeps them focused and, when necessary, can be used to call them back to their main role.

4. CLEARLY ESTABLISH REGULAR FEEDBACK LOOPS.

Annual or periodic reviews may be fine, but I'm a fan of more regular and informal feedback loops. Nobody wants to be left wondering if they're doing their job well. So in staff meetings, weekly check-ins, and intentional conversations, make a habit of encouraging people when they're working hard and executing well.

And when you observe something amiss, find the right time to address it. Ask questions. Probe. Pursue. And above all, be willing to have hard conversations. Don't cherish them, but don't run from them either. No one is perfect at their jobs, and it's the wise who through instruction gain knowledge (Prov. 21:11). And should the day ever come when you need to terminate a staff member for issues of character or competency, it should never come as a shock. If they're surprised, it means you've failed.

5. CLEARLY LEAD THROUGH HARD DECISIONS.

Ministry often feels like a parade of difficult conversations and decisions, especially for the lead pastor. It's why it's so critical that we fear God and not man. Fear man, and we'll be paralyzed by indecision. Fear God, and we're freed to move forward with charity, humility, and clarity.

This applies to staffing as well. Though it's a bit simplistic, I've found the old adage to hold true: "Be slow to hire, quick to fire." As the one at the head of the table, your elders and staff are looking to you to provide leadership and guidance.

And yet, as difficult decisions are made, don't make them alone. As much as possible, involve your elders. Talk through decisions with them. Help them understand. And if you ever must terminate a staff elder, make sure your lay elders not only understand but support the decision. That ought to be a decision you make with them.

6. BE PATIENT.

You may have built your staff. But many of us inherit staff, whose philosophy of ministry has been formed over years, often subconsciously. Therefore, it won't be reformed in days or weeks.

So be patient. Use staff meetings to instruct and reflect together. Constantly drip doctrine, watch, and pray. Look for who's humble and teachable. And as you lead, recognize everybody goes through hard seasons. Be patient. Remember they're people, not merely producers.

CONCLUSION

If the Lord gives you godly laborers who work diligently and humbly, then policies, hierarchies, formal reviews, and other "scaffolding" won't appear important. But sadly, no church is perfect. No staff is perfect. And no lead pastor is perfect. So may these encouragements bring further clarity, unity, and joy to your work.

ABOUT THE AUTHOR

Brad Wheeler is the senior pastor of University Baptist Church in Fayetteville, Arkansas.

What Job Titles Should Churches Use — Two Simple Rules

Jonathan Leeman

In case you missed it, the Southern Baptist Convention got into a bit of a tussle at this year's annual meeting over the definition of the word "pastor."

What provoked the tussle was the fact that in recent years Saddleback Community Church, a SBC church, installed several women as pastors. This seems to contradict the SBC's statement of faith, The Baptist Faith & Message 2000. It reads:

- a church's "scriptural officers are pastors and deacons";
- and "While both men and women are gifted for service, the office of pastor is limited to men as qualified by Scripture."

Contrary to bullet point 2, Saddleback has female pastors. Contrary to bullet point 1, they justify female pastors by dividing the pastoral office from the elder office. The question is then, should the SBC remove them from membership in the convention?

It's easy to fall into a debate over the second bullet limiting the office of elder to men. Yet often it's our treatment of the first line that creates the confusion about the second line.

Are there really only two offices in a church? If so, what do we make of a "minister of music" or a "children's director" or a "receptionist"? And what if a church distinguishes pastor from elder? Or what's the difference between a senior pastor and an associate pastor, or a mission's pastor and a youth pastor?

The larger question is, what job titles should churches use? Does the Bible care?

TWO OFFICES OR MORE?

For centuries Christians have disagreed on how many biblical offices there are and what they should be called. Since Calvin's day, Presbyterians have debated whether there are two offices or three (is the "teacher" different from the "elder"?). Most today say two.

Meanwhile, the first English Baptist confession, John Smyth's (1609), lists "bishops and deacons." The First London Confession of 1644 lists "pastors, teachers, elders, deacons," while the Second London Confession of 1688 returns to two: "bishops or elders and deacons." In fact, nearly all Baptist confessions mention only two, including the SBC's 1925, 1963, and 2000 Baptist Faith & Message, as we saw above.

The idea of two offices fits with Paul's greeting to the church in Philippi: "To all the saints in Christ Jesus who are in Philippi, *including the overseers and deacons*" (1:1). It also fits with the fact that he only lists qualifications for two offices—elders and deacons—in 1 Timothy 3.

To return to Saddleback, then, you can see how the two lines from the BF&M cited above implicate one another. For instance, when defenders of Saddleback's inclusion in the SBC argue that the line about men as pastors refers only to senior pastors (bullet point 2), they have placed themselves inside the centuries-old conversation about the number of offices (bullet point 1). Unwittingly or not, they're asserting that Scripture establishes three offices—senior pastor, pastor, and deacon—with different sets of qualifications and responsibilities.

The same trouble attends those who distinguish between elders and pastors, as Saddleback does. They've created a third office—elder, pastor, deacon.

The same is true for those who argue, in one breath, that the word "pastor" in the Bible does not refer to an authoritative *office* but to a *gift*, and in the next breath argue that this gift justifies the creation of what any innocent bystander would call...an office, complete with a name plate on the door. So, again, does the Bible call for two offices or three?

SO MANY TITLES

What complicates our present moment even further is how administratively complex and pragmatic some churches have become. To run a church of any size these days, you may well need what we call "a business administrator" and "a receptionist" and maybe a "director of children's ministry" and "youth pastor" and "minister of music" and "pastoral intern" as well as a "pastor of *this*," "*that*," and "*the other*." None of those titles are in the Bible. Doesn't that mean we should give up the game and go ahead and list as many offices as we need?

I don't think so. In spite of whatever titles we end up using (I'll say more about that in a moment), we should start by keeping the idea of two offices clearly separated in our minds for two reasons. First, God is wiser than man, and so we want to build our churches in accordance with the Scriptures.

Second, we should aspire to keep our church offices or jobs tied to biblical qualifications. Think about where Paul spills all his ink: a tiny bit on titles; a whole lot on qualifications. What does that tell us? We never want to go outside the qualifications he lists for those two offices. They're essential to a rightly "ordered" church (Titus 1:5).

As such, we should want basically everyone working in a titled capacity for a church, whether paid or unpaid, to meet the qualifications

- of a pastor or elder ("above reproach, the husband of one wife, sober-minded, self-controlled, respectable, hospitable, able to teach, not a drunkard, not violent but gentle, not quarrelsome" etc.)

- or of a deacon ("dignified, not double-tongued, not addicted to much wine, not greedy for dishonest gain…not slanderers, but sober-minded, faithful in all things" etc).

I'm pretty sure, for instance, you don't want someone answering the phone in your church office who is double-tongued and a slanderer. Right?

When we build church staffing structures that lose sight of these two basic offices, we risk untethering ourselves from their respective qualifications. It also leads us into the confusion we presently have over what men and women can or cannot do in a church. Folks have been quick to defend Saddleback's inclusion by saying, "Southern Baptists have meant a host of different things by the title 'pastor.'" That's true. We have. Which is why we're in this mess.

TWO SIMPLE RULES FOR DOCTRINAL CLARITY . . .

Let me offer two simple rules that should help our churches remain tied to Scripture while also offering some flexibility for different circumstances:

1) *Affirm that the Bible establishes two offices*[1] *and make sure that every titled job in a church, no matter what you call it, complies with the duties and qualifications of one or the other.*[2]
2) *Choose titles that reinforce the biblical division of labor and don't blur or confuse it, especially by paying attention to the nouns in those titles.*

So think back to my comment above about every position needing to meet the qualifications of a pastor or a deacon. Now let's take another step. I'm suggesting that

1 To be clear, the word "office" refers to a position

- given to certain named individuals, not the whole congregation,
- who meet certain qualifications,
- that gives them some type of authority either over the whole church or a specific area
- in order to fulfill certain responsibilities or functions.

2 Even if you don't think 1 Tim 3:10 refers to deaconess, the characteristics of these deacon wives could still be applied to female staff.

everyone with a title in a church (paid or unpaid) should essentially be slotted into one of two job descriptions broadly conceived:

- *Job description 1*: this person (i) possesses or shares oversight over the whole church (e.g., Acts 20:28; 1 Peter 5:1–5; Hebrews 13:7,17); (ii) is responsible for the ministry of the Word and prayer (e.g. Acts 6:1–7; 2 Tim. 2:1–2; 4:1–5; Titus 1:9; 2:1, 15; Heb. 13:7); and meets the qualifications set down by Paul in 1 Timothy 2:12 and 3:1–7 and Titus 1:5–9.
- *Job description 2*: this person (i) is a model servant (which is what the word "deacon" means); (ii) will attend to tangible needs, organize and mobilize acts of service, preserve the unity of the flock, and support the ministry of the elders (Acts 6:1–7);[3] (iii) and meets the qualifications set down by Paul in 1 Timothy 3:8–13.

For people in the first office, whether paid or unpaid, whether one person or several, whether affixed to an adjective like "senior" or "executive" or "young adult" or not, we should use the biblical nouns "pastor" or "elder" or "overseer" in the job title.

Locking down those three nouns to this first office will help our churches conform to the pattern of Scripture. And it will serve the purposes of clarity. Maybe *this* guy's day-to-day work is preparing sermons, *that* guy's is sitting in a counselor's chair, *that other* guy is leading mission trips, while *those* guys work all week in secular vocations but devote their evenings and weekends to shepherding sheep. Still, everyone in the church knows, "These are our spiritual overseers and shepherds. These are our pastors and elders. And they're all bound by the same qualifications."

Then, we can open our Bibles and read, "Remember your leaders, those who spoke to you the word of God. Consider the outcome of their way of life, and imitate their faith" (Heb. 13:7); and we can know how to apply it. We

3 The wording in this second clause is taken from Matt Smethhurst's book *Deacons* (Crossway, 2021).

can read a few verses later, "Obey your leaders and submit to them, for they are keeping watch over your souls, as those who will have to give an account" (v. 17); and we can know how to obey it. We're to follow the example of, we're to submit to, these men—our pastors or elders or overseers.

. . . AND CONTEXTUAL SENSITIVITY

Once that first office and the biblical nouns "pastor," "elder," and "overseer" are locked down, there's some flexibility with that second office and the job titles we might use for them. We might formally call such people deacons to recognize and affirm their model service. Yet we also might hire them as the church receptionist, children's ministry director, song leader, pastoral assistant, administrator, or building manager.[4]

Different circumstances call for different jobs, just like the challenge highlighted in Acts 6 concerning food distribution among widows was highly specific to that moment. The point is, all these jobs effectively place people into a diaconal role, as defined in job description 2 above. And with all these jobs I have difficulty imagining not asking them to meet the qualifications listed by Paul in 1 Timothy 3:8–13.

To be sure, some jobs in a church might feel like they fall somewhere in between descriptions 1 and 2. Maybe you have a "Christian Education Director" who is making decisions about what's taught in the Sunday School program and who is teaching the classes. My advice would be to push this individual more fully toward job description 1 or 2. Either recognize that he's already doing the work of a pastor by attending to what the church is taught, and so help the congregation recognize him as a pastor or elder as soon as possible. Or, if you're not convinced he's ready to be a pastor, make sure some pastor is overseeing his work. Your unwillingness to recommend him as a pastor means, to some extent, he's still working in a diaconal (assist the elders) capacity. And even if you

4 The title "minister" is tricky because different traditions use it for the pastor and other for something more diaconal. If you do use the term "minister" as a noun, aspire for clarity about what you're saying and what you're not saying.

trust his work entirely, the congregation has not yet entrusted their discipleship to his oversight.

PLEASE STOP CREATING LOOPHOLES OR BLURRING THE LINES

All that strikes me as pretty biblical and straightforward. Work hard at slotting every job into the pastoral or diaconal categories, and then make sure your job titles—especially the nouns—don't blur the assignments. Instead, restrict the nouns "pastor," "elder," and "overseer" to that first category. This creates flexibility in the second, which is useful since the focus of the second—tangible needs—will change from context to context.

Frankly, I think that counsel will serve both complementarian and egalitarian churches. It will help both clarify who they are and what they think biblical obedience requires. The churches this counsel will frustrate are those who are trying to land somewhere in between.

Which brings me to a final, more critical note. I'm struck by how often churches and writers end up creating loopholes by blurring the lines between these two offices.

Going back to the Saddleback conversation: To argue a woman can be a pastor but not the senior pastor is to create a loophole. You're blurring lines and fomenting confusion. Are you saying that "pastor" and "senior pastor" are different offices with different qualifications? Which biblical passages bind the one and which the other? And, if you think she can be affirmed as a pastor, why would you restrict her from preaching? That begins to feel arbitrary.

Or to argue that all the elders are pastors but not all the pastors are elders. How does that bring any clarity to the biblical job descriptions? As a member, am I to "obey and submit" in a Hebrews 13 way to both pastors and elders? If so, how do I relate to them differently? What passages should I consider? And, frankly, why the power differential between them? Is that just old-man elders trying to keep too much power from the young pastors they might hire?

Or to say, women cannot be pastors but they can be on the "leadership team." Wait a second:

what are the qualifications for the leadership team? Am I to submit to them? Do they possess oversight over the church, because the name certainly suggests they do?

All such fidgeting and blurring is confusing at best, misleading at worst. It would be clearer and better to simply say, "Women can be pastors or elders," if that's the road you want to take. The in-between stuff, increasingly common right now courtesy of these various loopholes, at least appears culturally motivated; more likely is the consequence of several decades of pastors learning to think pragmatically, not biblically.

The biblical patterns for church structures and leadership are meant to be a blessing. We shouldn't *want* to look for loopholes, like we do with our taxes. We should aspire to conform ourselves to the Bible and be clear about it.

APPENDIX: A FEW COMMENTS ON THE SBC-SADDLEBACK TUSSLE ITSELF

Since the article above raises the topic, I'd like to offer a few comments for my Southern Baptist friends on how we might navigate the SBC/Saddleback tussle itself.

If you google the story, you'll notice that reports often use the word "disfellowship" instead of "remove," as I did earlier. Should the SBC *disfellowship* Saddleback, people ask.

That's the wrong word to use, even if it's become the common way for SBCers to talk about removing a church from the convention. First, the SBC bylaws (correctly) don't use the word (see 8.C.2-5). More significantly, the Bible uses "fellowship" exclusively to refer to our gospel unity or fellowship, as when Paul refers to "the right hand of fellowship" (Gal. 2:9; see also, Acts 2:42, 2 Cor. 6:14; 1 John 1:3, etc.). To "disfellowship" a church, by that standard, would be to effectively excommunicate it, which Baptists don't believe conventions or denominations or presbyteries or general assemblies can do.

I trust that no one using the word "disfellowship" for or against Saddleback's membership means to suggest that excommunication is at stake. The trouble is folks then heap on other emotionally-laden language which raises the stakes almost that high. Disfellowshipping Saddleback would be a "tragedy," they say, and "grievous."

To which I can't help but respond, well, it's tragic only if we have an outsized view of God working exclusively among Southern Baptists. Doesn't he work outside the SBC, too? Can't Paul and Barnabas go separate ways and still both do great gospel work, and even bless each other as they go?

The question at play with Saddleback is not about *fellowship* but about *cooperating* or *convening* to train seminarians and send missionaries. This is why the Southern Baptist *Convention* exists. In a world of limited resources, my church can decide it does not want to pool resources with, say, the Presbyterians and Anglicans for missions, while still happily affirming our partnership in the gospel. In two weeks, I happen to be guest-preaching in a gospel-affirming Presbyterian church. Yet that doesn't mean I'd plant a church with them.

In that regard, denominational separations can, ironically, protect a deeper gospel unity. The alternative is to ignore or tut-tut secondary doctrinal matters (ordinances, church governance, women's ordination, etc.). Yet this leads to the potential for disobedience on both sides of a disagreement as well as to relativizing biblical authority, as in, "We need to obey *these* passages, but don't worry about *those*."

A better path may involve doing two things at once:

- separating denominationally, which heads off constant fighting and allows everyone to act according to their understanding of Scripture;
- looking for other ways (conferences, book projects, sharing pulpits, evangelizing together) to affirm our ongoing gospel partnership in primary matters.

Sometimes these amicable separations are the humbler path, particularly when nothing biblically sacrosanct is at stake, like a marriage vow. They acknowledge our fallenness and finitude and don't burden our consciences with the false weight of theological and ethical perfectionism.

As Christians more mature than me have said, we should work for peace amidst our disagreements on secondary matters by keeping the fences in between us clear but low; and shake hands over them often.

Imagine, then, the Saddleback conversation going like this. The SBC says to Saddleback, "We love you. Yet to allow both of us to hold our convictions regarding female pastors, we think it's best to separate. But we look forward to hearing reports of your ongoing gospel ministry and let us know how we can help."

To which Saddleback responds, "Makes sense, and we don't want to stir up controversy nor ask you to go against your conscience and understanding of Scripture. Pray for us, and we'll pray for you!"

That, to me, sounds like a mature conversation between two spiritually healthy adults.

ABOUT THE AUTHOR

Jonathan Leeman edits the 9Marks series of books as well as the 9Marks Journal. He is also the author of several books on the church. Since his call to ministry, Jonathan has earned a master of divinity from Southern Seminary and a Ph.D. in Ecclesiology from the University of Wales. He lives with his wife and four daughters in Cheverly, Maryland, where he is an elder at Cheverly Baptist Church.

Evaluating How an Elder Is Ruling

Bob Johnson

How do you conduct a job performance review for the elders (particularly the paid staff elders)? In other words, how do you determine if an elder is "ruling well"?

Before a man is considered for the office of an elder, he must be evaluated in light of the qualifications found in 1 Timothy 3 and Titus 1. But then what? Is that it? Is there anything in Scripture that suggests ongoing evaluation and encouragement for more effective ministry? Yes.

> "*Let the elders who rule well be considered worthy of double honor, especially those who labor in preaching and teaching*" (1 Tim. 5:17).

To consider an elder worthy of double honor, he must rule well. Paul's admonition indicates an evaluation process that determines whether he's doing this or not. Okay . . . But how? How can elders help one another "rule well"? How can a congregation know that its elders are serious about improving as elders?

Over the years, we've tried many ways to do "job performance evaluations," particularly for our staff elders. And I'm serious when I say *many*. Our efforts mostly returned empty. Sometimes, the process was so ponderous and frustrating that we just gave up for a while. Its value was overshadowed by what felt more business-like than biblical. However, after sustained effort, we've found an evaluation process that is workable—dare I say even good!

Here's what we did.

First, we asked each staff elder to come up with three questions for the rest of the elders to answer. We intended these questions to give each elder the chance to receive input into the areas he was most concerned about. For example…

- Where are my blind spots?
- How can I improve as a leader?
- What areas of ministry have lost traction under my authority?
- My wife says I can be aloof. Am I this way with the congregation?

Second, these questions were sent to every elder several days before we met to discuss them. This gave the brothers ample time to think and pray about their answers.

Third, the elders met to discuss our answers with one another, and we took notes on this conversation. We currently have 17 elders: six staff, eleven lay. Only the staff elders were evaluated. Knowing this meeting could drag on, we allotted 10 minutes to each staff elder. This may seem too brief, but the prep enabled effective, efficient conversation.

Fourth, each staff elder received a copy of everyone's answers. They were then asked to sign the document so we had a clear record of what had been agreed to.

I walked away encouraged, full of ideas for how I needed to improve. The other staff elders felt similarly. We all walked away built up, but with work to do. The process contributed to a culture of helping one another look more like Christ and enhanced our service to our church.

Our Administrative Pastor, Dave Kaynor, spear-headed this exercise. It was our best effort at a performance evaluation process, and I'm confident we'll repeat it next year.

ABOUT THE AUTHOR

Bob Johnson is the senior pastor of Cornerstone Baptist Church in Roseville, Michigan.

Why Clear Job Descriptions and Staff Structures Serve the Church

Ryan Townsend

Let's start with the big picture...

Every organization—from a Fortune 500 company to government bureaucracy to a non-profit—must define and align themselves according to four essential elements: strategy, operations, finances, and people. These decisions will determine how every organization will faithfully steward its resources and execute its mission.

- *Strategy* – This answers the identity question. Who are we? Why do we exist? What are our goals, objectives, purpose, vision, and mission? What key principles and core values define who we are (i.e., our "DNA")? The Bible has much to say about the church's strategy. The church is the body of Christ and ambassadors for King Jesus. Its strategy is the Great Commandment and the Great Commission.

- *Operations* – This answers the function question. Considering who we are (identity), what do we do? How do we operate? Again, the Bible answers these questions for the church. The church gathers to preach the Word, sing the Word, read the Word, pray the Word, and see the Word (i.e., practice the Lord's Supper and baptism). Practically, however, we need to figure how out these biblical values we budget and staff operate the church.
- *Finances* – Money is just fuel, but we must manage it well to execute our mission. After all, it doesn't grow on trees!
- *People* – People are at the heart of every organization, both on the outside and inside. For the church, staff—large or small—oversees and manages the shepherding, serving, and equipping of the congregation for Great Commission work (Eph. 4:11–16).

Of course, the church is different from any other organization on the planet. It's a blood-bought, supernatural creation that God himself creates (Eph. 2:1–22). But God uses pastors, deacons, and every member to do his work (Eph. 2:10; 4:11–16). And "success" in all this work is faithful stewardship (1 Cor. 4:1–2) of all God has entrusted to us. This is where we move from the big picture to everyday life.

Job descriptions and a clear org chart or staff structure are essential tools for organizational excellence and faithful management. They help keep those four essentials above in alignment through a five-fold purpose:

- Strategy - a good job description and org chart tie each position to the organization's vision, mission, purpose, and goals (i.e., the identity question). The job description details specifically and practically how each individual job serves the overall mission and goals most effectively and efficiently.
- Operations & Management – a good job description also helps to translate

the strategic value of a job into how the organization operates (i.e., answering the function question). Specifically, a good job description enables:

1. Planning – it prioritizes and schedules specific tasks and responsibilities.
2. Human resource administration – it serves as part of a job contract in many ways, detailing compensation, benefits, terms of employment, and work hours/schedule.
3. Clear operations – it defines and details expectations and tasks, along with the frequency and amount of time expected to do them.

- Training – a good job description is a key tool for training new staff. It provides all the key elements and details that must be addressed in staff transitions and training plans. It also serves current staff as a practical tool to monitor and manage their professional development, needs, goals, continuing education, etc.
- Evaluation – a good job description sets clear expectations and provides an objective standard to give and receive regular, specific feedback and performance reviews.
- Communication – a good job description helps the whole team understand what you do and how you fit into the organization. Since staff is often our most considerable expense, we need to communicate the tangible benefits and outcomes of staff positions so that our members understand their investment.

So, assuming you're convinced of its value, what are some critical pieces of a good job description?

JOB TITLE

A good job description should have a clear title.

JOB PROFILE

The job profile details the specific characteristics that best complement the particular tasks and responsibilities for the job. All job descriptions should have a brief description summarizing the ideal profile for the position.

The ideal job description highlights the importance of "the 4 Cs":

- **Character** – character is king. Bad character can be a team killer; good character, on the other hand, strengthens everyone around.
- **Competence** – do they have the skills and competencies necessary to do the job?
- **Communication** – are they able to communicate well with staff, members, and visitors?
- **Compatibility/Culture** – do they fit into the culture of your church staff/ membership?

JOB QUALIFICATIONS

This could complement or serve as the job profile. It provides specific qualifications and skills that are necessary for the job (e.g., communication, experience, relational, technical, travel, spiritual).

Relationships (i.e., clear staff structures)

The job description should clearly state whom the employee reports to, whom he/she works with, and, if applicable, who reports to him/her. This should parallel the org chart.

HOURS

This details the specific daily and weekly hours required for the job (e.g., 40–50 hours/week. Traditionally, Monday–Friday, 8:30-5:30 pm, and other times as needed).

RATIONALE

This briefly explains the big-picture/purpose behind the specific role, highlighting its strategic relationship and value-add to the church's mission and ministry. This may complement or be a part of the job profile.

Responsibilities

This breaks out in summary form the major categories/areas of responsibilities of the job.

DEPARTURE NOTICE

This explicitly explains the terms for notice and departure if the employee intends to leave the position.

THE ACTUAL, DETAILED JOB DESCRIPTION – SPECIFIC TASKS & RESPONSIBILITIES

This is by far the largest section of the job description. It takes the major responsibilities and spells out the specific expectations and individual tasks for the job. Depending on the nature of the role, you can use this section to explain the tools and processes to do each task. It's also generally helpful to include a note for each task that states the expected number of hours it should take.

In conclusion, remember that the job description is simply a tool to build up, encourage, and serve the whole staff and church. Therefore, while the core elements and responsibilities will stay the same in most roles, a good job description is a living document that you should review and revise regularly as the role innovates, grows, and changes.

ABOUT THE AUTHOR

Ryan Townsend is the Executive Director of 9Marks, and an elder at Capitol Hill Baptist Church in Washington, D. C.

Why Pastors Should Submit to Each Other

Jeff Wiesner

"Every leader is in some sense a follower. If a man does not follow, he cannot lead."

These words, spoken by a pastoral mentor, summarize the humble character of pastoral ministry. But unfortunately, it likewise exposes an endemic issue among disqualified pastors. They were taken down by a proud, authoritarian spirit that couldn't follow.

Such pride threatens every pastor's heart—the arrogant refusal to acknowledge God's goodness to limit his competency and authority. No pastor is omnicompetent. Nor is his authority absolute. Consequently, godly leaders must also be humble followers.

In this regard, every senior pastor should submit to several sources of authority: his Chief Shepherd (1 Pet. 5:4, Heb. 13:17), his own congregation (Matt. 18:17–20, Gal. 1:2, 6–9), his fellow elders (Acts 20:28), and the biblical standards for "life and doctrine", particularly those that are summarized in his church's governing documents (1 Tim. 4:7).

This article will focus on those latter two sources, demonstrating how *fellow elders* and *founding documents* guard a senior pastor against the pride of authoritarianism.

SUBMIT TO YOUR FELLOW ELDERS

Pastoral ministry is challenging. Satan is ferocious against God's church. False teachers, like ravenous wolves, devour it from the outside. Sin, like leaven, consumes it from within. These form the everyday context for pastoral ministry and inform Paul's final words to the Ephesians elders: "Pay careful attention to yourselves and to all the flock" (Acts 20:28).

The word translated "pay attention" carries the sense of being in a state of alertness or on guard. A church's elders cannot adequately guard the flock if they do not guard one another.

Moreover, this kind of guarding care is impossible without mutual submission. Each elder should entrust his life and ministry to fellow elders, and the senior pastor is no exception. But how can a pastor practically cultivate a leadership culture in which he is a leader *and* a follower?

1. Let Fellow Elders Guard Against Pride

"What three graces does a minister need most?"

Augustine famously replied, "Humility; humility; humility."

Tendencies toward heavy-handed pastoral leadership spring from the wicked pride of self-glory. C.S. Lewis described it as "the pleasure of being above the rest." Every pastor is vulnerable to this temptation and must heed Scripture's warnings, promises, and commands concerning sinful pride versus godly humility (Prov. 29:23; 1 Pet. 5:5–6; cf. Jas. 4:6).

These passages reveal that a genuinely humble pastor fears God above all. His chief aim in ministry is to glorify and enjoy God. He knows that a desire for God's glory fuels a holy motive to serve, while a lust for self-glory energizes a worldly desire to be served.

"Forget not," Abraham Booth wrote in his *Pastoral Cautions*, "that the whole of your work is ministerial; not legislative—that you are not a lord in the church, but a servant."

Godly elders must guard their church's senior pastor against pride, and he must submit to them. Relying on God's Word, fellow elders help a senior pastor measure himself against God's majesty They pray alongside him regularly, with thanksgiving (Phil. 4:6). He starves his ego by talking less during meetings and listening to fellow elders more, even at efficiency's expense. In short, when fellow elders serve and submit to one another, they suffocate authoritarian pride.

2. Lend Fellow Elders Your Ear

Senior pastors must also lend their ears to godly encouragement and criticism. Joel Beeke and Nick Thompson, in their helpful book *Pastors and Their Critics*, diagnose why this may be difficult for a pastor:

> The gospel-humble pastor will incline his ear. This is not something that comes easy for most pastors. We are used to doing the talking. Our job consists in an unending sequence of preaching, teaching, counseling, and giving advice.... We become very good at moving our mouths, but not so good at lending our ears.

Consider this statement in light of Jesus's words in Luke 8: "Take care how you hear" (v. 18). This recalls Jesus' earlier teaching: "As for the good soil, they are those who, *hearing* the word, hold it fast in an honest and good heart, and bear fruit with patience" (v. 15).

The tragic disqualifications of many talented preachers reinforce Jesus's point: a pastor's spiritual vitality and fruitfulness do not finally depend upon how well he *speaks* God's Word, but how well he *hears and obeys* it (cf. Heb. 5:11, Matt. 7:24–27).

Therefore, every pastor should "lend his ears" to his fellow elders. He must be humble in listening, teachable in receiving correction, and willing to submit to a brother's admonishment. Exemplary elders guard one another with their words *and* ears by speaking the truth in love to one another (Eph. 4:14–16).

Senior pastors, in particular, should create intentional spaces where they actively give and receive godly encouragement and criticism from fellow elders. These might include service reviews, off-the-record "executive sessions" in elder's meetings, or lunch and coffee meetings, to name a few possibilities.

In summary, elders cannot guard one another without mutual submission. Pastoral submissiveness requires godly humility. And this kind of humility compels a senior pastor to submit to fellow elders as they protect his life and ministry by speaking God's Word to him in spiritually beneficial ways.

SUBMIT TO YOUR FOUNDING DOCUMENTS

Even if a church has not yet recognized a plurality of elders, every senior pastor is accountable to his church's founding documents. Good founding documents summarize and apply the Bible's teaching on matters of sound doctrine (confession), godly living (covenant), and church polity (constitution).

When churches employ these in wise ways, a pastor becomes accountable to his congregation, and his congregation is protected from pastoral caprice. Specifically, a church's founding documents shape a pastor's ministry in three ways:

1. Teaching According to the Church's Confession

A church's confession is more than a page on their website and curriculum for their membership class. Much more, a confession says, "This is what we believe and how we interpret the Bible with other true churches around the world and through the ages."

Some may protest that using confessions in this way undermines *sola Scriptura.* But that's untrue. Scripture is supreme. A church's confession submits to Scripture. But a pastor's *interpretation* of Scripture submits to the confession.

I keep a copy of our church's confession within reach while preparing sermons for three reasons. First, it guards my teaching and preaching. Second, it allows me to bind my congregation to what they have already knowingly bound themselves. Third, it helps me promote charity and Christian liberty on disputable matters beyond our confession's scope.

In these ways, a confession protects congregations from being misled or wrongly bound by a pastor's individual, private interpretations of Scripture. Likewise, a pastor who submits to his church's confession can "watch his life and doctrine closely" and guard the integrity of his Word ministry (1 Tim. 4:16).

2. Living According to the Church's Covenant

Character is everything in pastoral ministry. The Bible encourages elders to be "examples to the flock" (1 Pet. 5:3). They are to be "above reproach" (1 Tim. 3:2). Paul told his pastoral protégé that "godliness is of value in every way" (1 Tim. 4:8; cf. 6:6).

If a church's confession summarizes sound doctrine, then a church's covenant summarizes a godly life. It encourages a congregation to grow in godliness and commends a pastor's exemplary character. Furthermore, it prevents pastors from turning right-and-left issues of Christian liberty into right-or-wrong matters of Christian obedience (e.g., alcohol, education, etc.).

My church's covenant explicitly commits me to Christian unity, love, holiness, evangelism, family worship, generosity, and more. So, as their pastor, I want to hold up our church covenant and say, "Brothers and sisters, follow me as I aim (always imperfectly) to follow Christ in these ways, by God's grace."

3. Ruling According to the Church's Constitution

A church's constitution is more than a legal document. It's a blueprint for a biblical polity that summarizes Scripture's teaching on how church membership and leadership work together to guard the gospel. How is church discipline to be executed? How are new elders and deacons affirmed? How do elder leadership and congregational authority practically work together?

The answers to these questions require prudential applications of Scripture, agreed upon by the congregation. A constitution describes how a church will *constitute* its life together. It's a manual for church polity.

Our church's elders put our constitution in front of our church as often as possible to prove ourselves above reproach and show our congregation we are not leading by *fiat*. For matters on which our church must vote—membership applications and resignations, elder and deacon nominations and affirmations, church discipline, etc.—we include the relevant portions of our church covenant in the member's meeting packet. Our goal is to equip our church to think well about biblical church polity and say to them, "Hey! We're not making this up as we go!"

How might pastoral authoritarianism be undermined if churches took their confession, covenant, and constitution seriously? These are good guides for godly leaders and healthy congregations. And senior pastors, above all, do well to submit to them.

ABOUT THE AUTHOR

Jeff Wiesner is the lead pastor of North Point Baptist Church in Denton, Texas. You can find him on Twitter at @jeffwiesner.

Buildings

ARE BUILDINGS ESSENTIAL TO HEALTHY CHURCHES?

Adam Sinnett

Are buildings necessary to building healthy churches? Does lacking a building put a church at a disadvantage? Does being mobile hinder disciple-making and the spread of the gospel?

THE DILEMMA EVERY PASTOR FACES

Every pastor I know whose church doesn't have a building wants one—and for good reason. Setting up and tearing down every Sunday is exciting, but only for a season. Recruiting faithful volunteers to arrive early and leave late—*every week*—is a challenge. Navigating relationships with landlords is often complex. Losing your space at the last minute is more common than you'd think. Finding a new space before the end of your current lease is time-consuming. This doesn't even include locating space for offices, classes, and mid-size gatherings throughout the week. This pastor is tempted to think, "If only we had a building . . ."

At the same time, almost every pastor I know whose church has a building, well, they want a slightly different one. After all, buildings can be too big or too small. The sanctuary may be just right, while there aren't enough classrooms. Or the kids' space may be ideal, but there aren't enough offices. Buildings are expensive to purchase, remodel, and maintain. Designated staff is typically required for facility management. The boiler always needs repair. (Why is it always the boiler?) Parking is usually a challenge, especially in urban contexts. This pastor is tempted to think, "If only our building had . . ."

PLACES AS STAGES

It's fascinating to survey the Scriptures and note the places where God tends to do redemptive work. Even a cursory reading reveals that God uses people in all kinds of places, from the everyday to the unexpected—from gardens, fields, arks, and prison cells to deserts, whale bellies, shipwrecks, and stables. But what's striking about this is that the places are always secondary. The places themselves are not the drama. They're merely the stages on which God's redemptive drama unfolds in ways big and small through the lives of his people.

So I wonder: why would we think it would be any different today? For those of us who may be tempted to think that God's work is somehow restricted or hindered by our space, we need this reminder.

THE PLACES OF DOWNTOWN CORNERSTONE

Our church gathers in the heart of downtown Seattle. We recently turned ten years old, and over the course of our shared life we've met in almost every conceivable type of space.

From birth to year four, our Sunday gatherings took place in a basement-level antique shop, then an office building foyer, and then a movie theater (in fact, we met in five different theaters in the same complex over three years). We used conference rooms for classes. We offered pre-marital counseling in living rooms. We had prayer nights in a local community center. Our small groups met in condos, on rooftops, and throughout parks. Early morning discipleship groups met in cafes. Our staff worked out of a shoebox sized office that had been donated to us.

And yet, Jesus used these scattered, everyday places as stages on which to spread the gospel, save sinners, and sanctify his people.

From year four to the present, we've leased a former dance club. This was incredibly significant for our fledgling church. It gave us a more permanent presence in our community. There was no more set-up and tear-down. We could consolidate all our ministry efforts to one central location.

But . . . our sanctuary is too small, our office space is too limited, and we're kept from making any improvements by our landlords. Our family entrance is literally in an alley. We're glad to be in the most densely populated neighborhood downtown. But this area also attracts graffiti, urine, and drug deals. Oh, and did I mention it has no windows?

And yet Jesus is using this imperfect building as a stage on which to spread the gospel, save sinners, and sanctify his people.

From the beginning, we prayed, searched, and saved for a permanent building. We continually found ourselves coming up short. Some buildings were too small. Others were too expensive. Most were located outside the city center. Still others were purchased in cash by developers before the ink was dry on our own offer. But by God's grace, after ten years of searching and saving, we purchased a building in December 2020. While this is a huge piece of evidence of God's grace toward us, we now find ourselves leading a capital campaign and a building project. Meanwhile, amid a once-in-a-century pandemic, the cost of raw materials has soared.

Buildings are a gift, but they too have their challenges.

THE ADVANTAGES/ DISADVANTAGES OF NOT HAVING A BUILDING

Here are a few *advantages* of being mobile:

- Your church isn't tied down to a particular place.
- There's no financial burden of a mortgage.
- As your church grows, you can simply move to a larger space.
- Generally, your landlord is responsible for facility repairs.

But there are, of course, some *disadvantages*:

- Your experience will often be determined by your landlord.
- Set up and tear down requires significant energy and volunteer capital.
- You will often be thinking about where to meet next.
- Lacking a permanent space can communicate a lack of rootedness to the community.

THE ADVANTAGES/ DISADVANTAGES OF HAVING A BUILDING

Here are a few *advantages* of owning a building:

- A permanent building communicates stability and presence.
- You no longer need to set up and tear down every week.
- You no longer need to be concerned with lease negotiations, landlords, or finding new spaces.
- Your church is usually easier to find.
- You have more freedom to make facility improvements.

But there are some *disadvantages*, too:

- Buildings can be expensive and require ongoing repair.
- They often need staff attention.
- If the building is too small, you'll need to find another space or invest in an expensive renovation.
- If the building is too big, your church may have difficulty supporting it.
- If it's in a poor location, it may not serve the church well.

CONCLUSION

So, are buildings essential to building healthy churches? No. Can they be incredibly helpful? Absolutely.

Is God's work limited by your space? No. Does having a building guarantee more fruitfulness? No. Does a building make all your physical space issues go away? No.

Now here's the trickiest question: should a church get a building if it can? In most cases, I'd say yes. The benefits outweigh the burdens. Above all, whether we have a building or not, we need to remember that our space is merely one stage on which God's redemptive drama continues to unfold.

ABOUT THE AUTHOR

Adam Sinnett is the lead pastor of Downtown Cornerstone Church in Seattle, Washington.

The Benefits of Having a Building

Benjamin Woodward

Today, the Dubai skyline offers an impressive row of towering skyscrapers, world-class hotels, and the world's tallest building. On the south side of the city sits our humble church home.

While unimpressive by architectural standards, this church building is priceless. It's the only building licensed by the government for evangelical Christian worship in our city of nearly three million people. Currently, just three other evangelical church buildings exist in the entire country of UAE. Each week, our building in Dubai hosts more than a dozen congregations which speak Arabic, Urdu, Chinese, Korean, Telugu, Tagalog, Hindi, and English, and in so doing it facilitates the gathered worship of thousands of evangelical believers from more than 70 nations.

We often tell our congregations that the church is not a building but a body: a blood-bought community of the redeemed. We stress this because conflating the church with a building is common and yet destructive to the church's true identity and mission. Buildings can become distractions from the gospel; they can even become idols.

But just because a good thing is corruptible doesn't mean it's not a good thing. In fact, a church is not just a people; it's a people constituted as a people by gathering in a place. Without some place to gather, like a building, scattered saints cannot become a church.

A building set apart for gospel use is a gracious gift from God, one that's often been given through the sacrifices of previous generations. We too easily overlook or even grumble about what we should be thankful for.

As believers, our physical bodies matter. Genesis teaches this, and the incarnation confirms it. Similarly, a church is an assembly of embodied creatures who gather weekly because of the gospel and to be built up by that same gospel. So it's no surprise that believers through the centuries have created designated spaces for gathered, regular worship—whether in homes, catacombs, or distinct church buildings.

FOUR BENEFITS OF A CHURCH BUILDING

1. Maximizing Word Ministry

The church grows in size and maturity as the gospel brings faith and conforms us into Christ's image. This does not require a building, but a building supports the ministry of the Word.

With a dedicated building, the space can be optimized for preaching, teaching, and fellowship. The sound system can be prepared and ready. People know where to gather each week and how to get there. The HVAC system can mitigate bad weather and allow people to focus on the prayers, song lyrics, and sermon. Appropriate classrooms can be prepared for each specific need. Simply put, more people can benefit from the preaching and teaching of the Word when a space is optimized for this purpose.

A meeting space can be a distraction when the aim is entertainment or fostering a mystical experience. So we should design our spaces to center the congregation's attention on the living and active Word of God because God has promised it will not return void. This reconfiguration of church buildings and worship halls occurred during the Protestant Reformation. Reformers placed the pulpit in the center, replacing the table for the Lord's Supper. A building is a strategic part of a church's trellis that can be intentionally shaped to support vine growth.

2. Stability for the Long-Term

The church is a collection of sojourners, but stability for gospel ministry is a welcome blessing. Some church leaders, especially in missions' contexts, argue that believers should avoid becoming distracted by buildings because buildings can't be replicated quickly enough. Such proposals are short-sighted. There is nothing strategic about a congregation being uncertain of where it will meet next month, or if they may be kicked out of their space, or if neighbors may complain if the congregation doubles in size.

Buildings promote stability and give greater freedom to gospel ministry. There are seasons and places where a dedicated church building is simply unavailable. But when such a building is available, a congregation can better sink deep roots into its neighborhood and community.

For its first 25 years, our congregation in Dubai gathered in schools and private homes. God provided what we needed for this season, but there were many challenges, too. After years of praying, HH Sheikh Hamdan bin Rashid Al Maktoum granted land for an evangelical church building in 1997. This grant of land and the building we built has given us the stability we needed for greater member care, training pastors, planting churches, and visibility to our witness. Speaking of…

3. *Public Gospel Witness*

A church's public identity in a city is a persistent witness to the gospel. House churches are generally invisible, often intentionally. Again, this can be necessary at times. But the church should aspire to foster a corporate, public testimony to the gospel.

A few years ago bus routes were redrawn in our neighborhood, and the new bus stop in front of our church building was named "The Evangelical Church." We were honored! Each Christmas, the ruler of another emirate graciously fixes Christmas lights in the parking lot of the Evangelical Church there. Before Easter, the local police strategize with us on how to manage the increased traffic.

Being a small Christian minority in an Islamic country, we're glad to be recognized as a community fixture. Attempting to worship in secret could suggest we have nefarious and ulterior motives. Gathering publicly in an identifiable church building announces that we are Christians gathering to worship our Savior. We are glad to be a landmark for the curious in our city who want to understand more about the Bible, Jesus Christ, and our faith.

4. Cost Savings

Building projects require significant capital investment. On-going maintenance takes up valuable staff time and requires allocations from the annual budget.

But these costs are long-term investments in the ministry of the church. Short-term rental agreements and changing plans cost even more. When churches engage in building projects and upkeep wisely, the congregation can focus its financial resources on gospel work near and far that will have an impact in eternity. It also saves money for future generations of church members who can continue to make good use of the building.

CONCLUSION

The church in my region of the world is small, but it still contains evidence of the vibrant Christian faith of previous generations. I've walked through the ruins of a large basilica dating to fifth century Carthage (present-day Tunis) as well as the Hagia Sophia, constructed by emperor Justinian in sixth century Constantinople (present-day Istanbul). And on a small island off the coast of Abu Dhabi, near the border with Saudi Arabia and Qatar, sits the ruins of a Christian church and monastery from the seventh century. Although none of these ruins are used for Christian worship now, they testify to the Christian congregations and faith present in North Africa and the Middle East before the arrival of Islam.

If your church owns a building, give thanks to God, and remind your congregation to do so. Despite their quirks and faults, our buildings promote health and growth in our gatherings, while the gatherings testify to the communities around us that Christ is our risen Lord.

ABOUT THE AUTHOR

Benjamin Woodward is an associate pastor of the Evangelical Christian Church of Dubai.

What to Do When Your Building Is Full

Mike Carnicella and Greg Gilbert

What's the correct size for a church? Is it possible for a church to be too big? What happens when a church grows to the point it no longer fits in one building? Here's the popular answer: start another service. But let's assume you are committed to one service only. Your building is full on Sunday. Now what?

The first thing to do is examine all the options. Assuming you've ruled out multiple services or multi-site, then there are really only four choices.

Option 1: Do nothing.

Pretty self-explanatory.

Option 2: Carve off part of the church and send them out to do a church plant or church revitalization.

Note: A variation of this option would include carving off part of your church and having them meet in the same building, but at a different time. You might be thinking to yourself, "That sounds like multiple services." That's true; it does sound like it. But if the second gathering has its own pastors and distinct membership, then you actually have two churches meeting in the same building. One church with multiple services is an oxymoron since the essence of the church is to gather.

Option 3: Move to a different building and location.

Option 4: Renovate or add on to your existing building.

Here are several factors to consider when deciding what to do when you run out of room.

CONSIDERATIONS

The Strengths and Weakness of Buildings

Buildings have benefits and costs. Be aware of both.

Costs: they break and require maintenance. Over time, they can become an idol, a distraction, or a museum.

Benefits: over time, church-in-a-box is taxing to a congregation. Just ask any church plant who has been meeting in a school gymnasium for more than a few months. Buildings are more likely to enable a generational church; and they offer a standing invitation to the community.

The Unpredictability of Attendance

It's hard to predict the size of a church and attendance on any given Sunday. So a building that allows some flexibility is helpful. We have an overflow room that we use strategically during our predictable weeks of highest attendance each year (our adult attendance can fluctuate from 400 all the way to 750 because of our proximity to schools and universities).

Packed Is Better than Potential

A crowded room is better than a sparse room. We could rent the Kentucky Convention Center and have plenty of room to grow, but our 700 people would suddenly seem quite small—and maybe a little pathetic.

No Solution Is Final

There's no silver bullet here. If the Lord gives growth, you'll eventually face the same questions with a church of 1500 as you did with 200. Don't look for one solution for the ages. Solve one problem, then solve it again a few years from now if necessary.

OUR STORY

So, given all that, what do you do?

This is a live question for us at Third Avenue. We inherited a decrepit building that had seating for around 250 on the main floor and another 200 in the balcony, if renovated. In 2010, there were around 100-150 people attending Sunday morning. Today, we are a church of around 750 members, and we have a main hall that seats around 675. Along the way, we chose to do incremental renovations that gave us the opportunity to keep growing. But now we are up against the wall, and we're facing the same dilemma. We've looked at all the options and even sent dozens of members to both church plants and church revitalizations over the last few years. But we're still growing, and we have no more room in our building.

So what do we do?

Plant another church! That's the obvious answer, right? For a variety of reasons, we've decided that it's worth it to plan another renovation that would allow us to double our size from 750 to 1400 members, even though it will cost us upwards of $10 million. *Gasp!* But we think it will be worth it. Why?

We've thought about moving locations, but we don't think that would be best for our church. We've thought about big church plants, but again, we don't think that would be the best thing for us to do right now. We want to affirm that we think church planting is both biblical and necessary. It's a good thing! However, based on our experience and observations of churches in a similar position, we don't think church planting is the answer to our space problem. We believe you should plant a church when there is a good, strategic reason to do so.

WHY NOT PLANT?

Why have we decided that planting a series of churches isn't the next move for us? Here are a few reasons.

1. Resources

Large churches can do lots of good ministry. Believe it or not, bigger churches can do even more ministry. They can plant more churches, do more outreach, and train more people for ministry than an equal number of people divided into three or four churches. That's in part because of the often-overlooked fact that a large church will likely have much less overhead than, say, four smaller churches.

There are potential drawbacks that come with a church that continues to grow, of course. One possible difficulty is keeping track of more and more sheep. But for us, having grown from 100 to 750 over the last 10 years, that's not our experience.

One marker we have tracked over the years is attendance at our evening service, which is a completely different service from the morning. It has a less formal feel and gives new members a chance to connect on a deeper level. As we've grown over the years, we've actually seen attendance at our evening service go up from 30 to 40 percent when we had 200 members to more like 50 to 60 percent now that we have 750.

Thankfully, we haven't also seen an increase in church discipline cases on a percentage basis. Keeping track of the sheep is a high priority and something we keep a close eye on, and we're confident that continued growth won't cause us to compromise in this area.

Another common objection we hear is that when the church is larger, an individual member can no longer deeply know everyone in the church. That's true, but it was true even when we were a church of 150 members. No matter how big your church is, especially once you get bigger than about 50 people, each individual member simply can't know everyone the same. There will always be members you know on a deeper level and others you know on a shallower level. You can't be best friends with everyone in the church, and that's not the point of the church anyway.

2. Church Planting Isn't Simple

Second, at least for us, we can't plant churches fast enough to deal with our space problem. Church planting is a complex endeavor. You need to think through leadership, finances, and who will form the church. All of that takes a significant amount of time and resources to pull off well.

It may be different for your church, but for us, planting a church of 100-150 people every year is not something we are currently able to do. But that's what would be needed to deal with our space problem.

3. Church Plants Should Be Healthy

Third, and relatedly, we're not interested in just planting churches. We want to plant *healthy* churches. That means, among other things, we want the churches we plant to last for a long time. We're not interested in planting a bunch of churches and hoping that some percentage of them will survive and thrive. We believe that successful church plants require significant leadership and resources, both of which are hard to come by.

On top of that, you need a new church to be comprised of healthy members, so we want those members to have been around long enough to absorb our ecclesiological DNA and be able to stay with the church plant for a while.

A quick look at the regular turnover of our membership reveals that the average church member only stays 3 to 4 years. In other words, we turn over 75 percent of our membership every 3 to 4 years! Why such drastic turnover? Because a large percentage of our members are here for school, and they plan to go somewhere else when they finish their studies. While we're thankful that those members are with us during that time, people who are only planning to be in town for a few years aren't exactly prime candidates for the core of a church plant. But if we were a church of 1400 instead of 750, then we could plant a church comprised of longer and shorter-term members without compromising the core of our own church.

CONCLUSION

Again, planting churches is a good and worthy thing to do. But a big, Bible-believing church is good, too! Your situation and analysis may differ, but we believe we can do more training, church planting, and missions from a larger base.

Each church will face different decisions and obstacles when it begins to run out of space, and each church must make its own decisions. But in the end, the goal—for all of us—is to follow Jesus's marching orders to make disciples of our Lord. To God be the glory!

ABOUT THE AUTHORS

Mike Carnicella is an associate pastor for administration of Third Avenue Baptist Church in Louisville, Kentucky.

Greg Gilbert is the Senior Pastor of Third Avenue Baptist Church in Louisville, Kentucky. You can find him on Twitter at @greggilbert.

A Theological Framework for Buildings and Renovations

John Henderson

As we continue in a season of hiring architects and contractors to evaluate our facilities and recommend steps toward building and renovating facilities, it seems prudent to discuss and develop our theology of buildings. The goal as elders will be to wisely avoid two ditches:

1. *Glorying in our buildings* (a form of materialism) — where we measure our church health by buildings, or measure the Lord's faithfulness to us by the quality of our buildings, or boast in our buildings before others, or find encouragement for gospel ministry from our buildings.
2. *Despising our buildings* (a form of asceticism) — where we measure our spiritual maturity by how happy we are with dilapidated buildings, or boast in our old facilities, or equate physical

renovations and construction with worldliness, or wrongly accuse God of judging churches who improve their facilities.

Along with avoiding these ditches, we also want to develop a positive, biblical understanding of physical resources in fulfilling our calling as ambassadors for Christ and ministers of the gospel. We don't want to be dependent upon buildings, but we do want to utilize every resource the Lord provides in honoring his name and bearing fruit as his church. We want to be good stewards. We want to be a church who walks wisely and faithfully through building projects. We want to understand from Scripture a theology of church property, facilities, and physical resources.

I. A THEOLOGY OF BUILDINGS

1. The Significance of Physical Places in Scripture

The physical world was created good, not evil, and can been used for good or evil. Even more, the Lord has used physical places in the created world for significant purposes.

1. Pillars and altars (Genesis 12:7-8; 22:9-14; 28:10-22; 2 Samuel 24:18-25)
2. The tabernacle (Exodus 24:15-25:9; 40:34-38)
3. The Promised Land (Exodus 32:11-14; Joshua 4:1-7)
4. Jerusalem (Nehemiah 1:8-10)
5. The temple (1 Kings 8:1-11; 2 Chronicles 7:11-12)
6. Jesus Christ taking on human flesh (John 1:1-14)
7. Our bodies (1 Corinthians 6:17-20)
8. The church, the body of Christ (1 Corinthians 12:12-31)
9. The new heavens, new earth, new Jerusalem (Revelation 21)

There is clearly a shift in emphasis on physical places and buildings as Scripture progresses. The Old Testament is full of physical shadows and types that were meant to prepare the people of God for the coming of their Messiah. The entire sacrificial system was fulfilled in Jesus Christ. The physical temple in Jerusalem gave way to the church-as-temple-of-God under the new covenant. He dwells in a people, not a building. The conversation between Jesus and the woman at the well signaled a marked transition.

Jesus said to her, "Woman, believe me, the hour is coming when neither on this mountain nor in Jerusalem will you worship the Father. You worship what you do not know; we worship what we know, for salvation is from the Jews. But the hour is coming, and is now here, when the true worshipers will worship the Father in spirit and truth, for the Father is seeking such people to worship him. God is spirit, and those who worship him must worship in spirit and truth." (John 4:21–24)

Of course, the Lord is not done with physical spaces. There will be a new heavens and earth, a new Jerusalem, and all kinds of glorious physical spaces in the eternal state, and we're meant to be excited about it. Though the sacrificial system and physical temple of the OT was fulfilled in Christ and his church, they also represented and reflected the reality of heaven in various ways. Moses was to build the Tabernacle to the exact design God provided because it would be a copy of the real thing in heaven.

2. What Happens in the Physical Place Is the Essential Thing

Consider God's words through the prophet Haggai:

In the seventh month, on the twenty-first day of the month, the word of the Lord came by the hand of Haggai the prophet: "Speak now to Zerubbabel the son of Shealtiel, governor of Judah, and to Joshua the son of Jehozadak, the high priest, and to all the remnant of the people, and say, 'Who is left among you who saw this house in its former glory? How do you see it now? Is it not as nothing in your eyes?

Yet now be strong, O Zerubbabel, declares the Lord. Be strong, O Joshua, son of Jehozadak, the high priest. Be strong, all you people of the land, declares the Lord. Work, for I am with you, declares the Lord of hosts, according to the covenant that I made with you when you came out of Egypt. My Spirit remains in your midst. Fear not. For thus says the Lord of hosts: Yet once more, in a little while, I will shake the heavens and the earth and the sea and the dry land.

And I will shake all nations, so that the treasures of all nations shall come in, and I will fill this house with glory, says the Lord of hosts. The silver is mine, and the gold is mine, declares the Lord of hosts. The latter glory of this house shall be greater than the former, says the Lord of hosts. And in this place I will give peace, declares the Lord of hosts.'" (Haggai 2:1-9)

God uses physical buildings. The glory of a building does not rest in the size, style, and opulence, but in how God uses it to accomplish his purposes. In the days of Zerubbabel, some people mourned, and some rejoiced at the sight of the new temple, mostly for the wrong reasons. The Lord wanted them to grasp what mattered most. Jesus Christ would someday step into that very temple. The Son of God would take on flesh, enter Jerusalem, and bring peace.

Of course, even the new temple would not last. Jesus Christ announced its destruction: "Jesus left the temple and was going away, when his disciples came to point out to him the buildings of the temple. But he answered them, 'You see all these, do you not? Truly, I say to you, there will not be left here one stone upon another that will not be thrown down'" (Matthew 24:1-2). The temple served a purpose, and then it was destroyed. Another temple was built, the body of Christ, the Church, filled with the Spirit of God.

3. The Church Is a People, Not a Building

Union with Christ through the indwelling of the Holy Spirit, who unites us to Christ, is one of the glorious truths of the gospel (Galatians 2:20; 1 Corinthians 6:17-20). Even more, we are joined to one another because of our union with Christ. The church, therefore, is composed of people. We are the stones of a new temple for the glory of God, and Christ is the cornerstone:

> As you come to him, a living stone rejected by men but in the sight of God chosen and precious, you yourselves like living stones are being built up as a spiritual house, to be a holy priesthood, to offer spiritual sacrifices acceptable to God through Jesus Christ (1 Peter 2:4-5).

4. Our Primary Work Is Spiritual, Not Physical

The Lord Jesus Christ commissioned us to make disciples, not buildings: "All authority in heaven and on earth has been given to me. Go therefore and make disciples of all nations, baptizing them in the name of the Father and of the Son and of the Holy Spirit, teaching them to observe all that I have commanded you. And behold, I am with you always, to the end of the age" (Matthew 28:18-20).

The apostle Paul purposely came to the Corinthians, not with the wisdom of the world, but with Christ and him crucified, "in the demonstration of the Spirit and of power," through lives transformed by the gospel. It makes sense to extend his reasoning to buildings. We preach Christ and view lives transformed by the power of God through the gospel to be evidence of fruitfulness, not buildings.

5. Buildings Are Helpful, Not Essential

It is wise to conclude that we do not *need* church buildings. If a day arises when we lose our church property, the church will remain and, by God's grace, thrive. The gates of Hades shall not prevail against the church of Jesus Christ (Matthew 16:18).

At the same time, church buildings are helpful. If the Lord allows, we are wise to take advantage of every resource we receive in the ministry of the gospel and the edification of his church. Though we could say much about the wise use and purpose of church property and buildings, the following section will highlight a few ways our buildings help us fulfill the mission to which Christ calls us.

II. OUR PURPOSE FOR BUILDINGS

As previously stated, church property and buildings are not essential, but they can be helpful. They are not evil, though they can be built and used for evil reasons. They can be distracting and tedious, but they can also be useful in obeying the Great Commission.

Behind our theology of church property is our theology of all created things. They are gifts from the Lord that may be used rightly or wrongly, for the glory of Christ or the glory of mankind. We probably need continual reminders about the purpose of physical things, which are to be received humbly and with genuine thanksgiving. They should be used in service to Christ and his kingdom, for the ministry of the gospel, for the love of people. If we keep viewing them as mere means by which we fulfill our mission as a church, then we will probably stay on a good track.

1. A Place to Assemble in the Worship of our Great God, Minimizing Distractions Where Possible (Snow and Rain; Noise; Intense Cold or Heat, etc.)

Though we could break into 20 small churches meeting in houses, overseen by 20 separate groups of elders, our building provides the opportunity to meet as one local church bearing one witness to the surrounding world led by one group of elders.

A building also helps us focus the resources of the Lord with precision and wisdom. When we gather in one place at one time, the church can be built up through the ministry of one pastor preaching one sermon, through the ministry of one music team leading the singing.

A building allows us to worship God together. It allows us to break bread together at one time. It protects our bodies from rain and snow in order to hear the preaching of the Word, pray as a congregation, and worship the Lord with minimal distractions. It provides a space for members of our congregation to encourage, strengthen, serve, and love one another.

2. A Place to Equip the Saints for the Work of Ministry (Classrooms; Fellowship Halls; Children's Ministry Rooms)

For the most part our paid pastors and staff have an office at the church, which is very helpful for preparing sermons, counseling members, and teaching Bible studies. When Paul preached at Ephesus, he was not received in the synagogue, but he was able to "reason daily in the hall of Tyrannus" (Acts 19:9). For approximately two years Paul preached, taught, and made disciples in that building. I'm sure he was very thankful for it.

3. A Place to Help Us Make Disciples of Jesus Christ as Well as Train Future Pastors and Leaders in the Work

The church property and buildings allow us to overcome certain obstacles to ministry, like meeting space constraints, parking constraints, cost of utilities, etc. For example, if housing is a significant obstacle for future pastors and church leaders to receive training at DRBC, and the Lord provides means to remove those obstacles, then it may be wise to do so.

4. A Visible Mark of the Church

Strangers can walk in. People driving by can see and inquire. People can see and hear the church being the church together because we have a place to gather in one accord. Though the church is a people, not a building, these people show themselves as the church when they gather together in worship, service, and care for one another.

The Lord uses our unity, Christ-centered lives, and proclamation of the gospel to bear witness to the world. It helps, at the same time, when we have a place where people can walk in from the street and actually witness our unity, Christ-centered lives, and gospel proclamation. Again, a building is not essential, but it is helpful to this end.

We encourage you to take time in the days ahead to read some of the passages in this document and pray for the Lord to give us wisdom in developing and renovating our buildings. If other passages of Scripture come to mind that might be helpful as we think about buildings and renovation, then please send those passages and ideas to the elders.

EDITOR'S NOTE

The following is a document produced by the elders of Del Ray Baptist Church in Alexandria, VA to instruct their congregation on how to think about upcoming building renovations.

ABOUT THE AUTHOR

John Henderson is the Associate Pastor of Counseling and Family Ministries at University Baptist Church in Fayetteville, Arkansas.

Budgeting

HOW TO TALK WITH YOUR CHURCH ABOUT MONEY

Jamie Dunlop

Do you enjoy talking with your church about money? For many pastors, almost anything else would be preferable. Too often, it seems the moment you start talking about money, all the air is sucked out of the room.

"Here goes the pastor again, laying on the guilt. Time to check out."

How can discussing money with your church become a positive experience for them and for you? Let's see how the apostle Paul discussed money, and then apply his approach to scenarios you may find yourself in.

THE STRANGEST THANK YOU NOTE

Paul ends his delightfully encouraging letter to the Philippians by thanking them for their recent gift. But this doesn't look anything like the thank you notes you receive from your favorite charity: "Thank you for your recent gift; we could never do this important work without you; here are 17 more needs we have; could you please give more?"

Instead, Paul bends over backward to make it clear that God's work is in no way dependent on their generosity. "Not that I am speaking of being in need, for I have learned in whatever situation I am to be content"

(Phil. 4:11). "I can do all things through him who strengthens me" (4:13). "Not that I seek the gift . . . I am well supplied" (4:17-18).

Nonetheless, Paul "rejoices" in their gift (4:10). Why? Not for his sake, but for theirs. "Not that I seek the gift, but I seek the fruit that increases to your credit" (4:17). As it turns out, Paul really believed those words of Jesus he quoted in Acts 20:35, "It is more blessed to give than to receive." According to Paul, giving is for the benefit of the giver.

Here are a few principles we can take from Paul's example:

1. When we talk about money with our congregations, we should exemplify an exuberant confidence that God in his providential care for our churches will provide exactly what is right, whether or not that amount is what we'd hoped for.
2. When we talk about money, our primary interest is the eternal good of our sheep, not the plans of their shepherds.
3. Talking about money is an opportunity to teach our people how to think about money.

SPEAKING LIKE PAUL

Consider a few scenarios churches face and how we can discuss money like Paul when they occur.

When Asking Your People to Give

Every pastor should teach about giving. It's a topic that's covered repeatedly in Scripture. When you do, follow Paul's example by making it clear that you're not teaching about giving because your church needs the money; you're teaching about giving because it's good for your congregation to give. Giving loosens their heart's grasp on the things of this world (Matt. 6:21); giving is an investment in an eternal reward (Phil. 4:17).

When You Present the Budget

Paul's example inclines us to describe the church budget less as spending and more as investment. In that regard, you might describe your church's budget as a spiritually oriented mutual fund.

In a financial mutual fund, thousands of investors entrust their money to an investment manager, who looks for the best opportunities to invest that money, so that someday people will see a return on their investment. Likewise, your congregation entrusts to your church a significant portion of their wealth each year. Your church "invests" that money in kingdom-oriented work, like paying pastors and funding missionaries. One day, each of these saints will stand before God to give account for how they stewarded what he entrusted to them (2 Cor. 5:10). Let's pray that on the last day, they are grateful for every bit of money they gave to your church budget.

When Your Church Is Doing Well Financially

We often don't talk as much about money when the church is doing well financially, but that's the *best* time to talk about giving—precisely because it's when our motives are least likely to be misunderstood. I often say something like, "I'm thankful our church is doing well financially, but frankly, I couldn't care less whether or not we meet our budget. Instead, what I care about is you: the state of your heart, the opportunity for giving to free you from worldly concerns, and the reward that awaits faithfulness. In fact, the reason I'm mentioning this now is precisely because we *are* meeting our budget."

When Your Church Is Behind Budget

When times are tight, make it clear you love your people far more than you love your budget-dependent plans. You will need a healthy dose of faith-filled confidence in the providential care of a good and sovereign God. As David wrote, "The boundary lines have fallen for me in pleasant places; surely I have a delightful inheritance" (Ps. 16:6). That is *always* true—whether God has provided 110% of your budget or 10%. As you speak from such confidence, not only will you show by example what it looks like to trust God's good purposes in hard providence, but your people will more easily trust that your desire is not their money, but the good of their souls.

Of course, saying the words "I care much more about your faithfulness than about meeting this budget" can ring hollow if the congregation knows your back is against the wall and you'll need to lay off staff unless more money comes in. So avoid having your back against the wall! How? By maintaining some flexibility in your budget. For example, if possible, save some lines (say, for discretionary building improvements or one-time missions' opportunities) that you don't spend until the end of the fiscal year. Budget flexibility will go a long way toward helping your congregation trust that you care more about their souls than their money.

When You're in a Time of Financial Emergency

No matter how wise your planning, there will be times when your back is, indeed, against the wall, and you will have to make some painful decisions unless your congregation increases their giving. My advice in these situations? Be honest: "Almost always when I encourage you to give, I'm doing so not because of our budget, but because of your hearts. Like Paul in Philippians 4, I'm seeking the fruit that increases to your credit. But this time is different. I'd hate for us to cut long-term investments in staff and missionaries in order to accommodate what I believe to be a short-term financial crisis. So I'm asking you to give beyond what is faithful. If we can balance our budget, I think it will be a better spiritual investment vehicle over the long run. And if we can't, that's OK—we know God will provide exactly what we need."

Who Talks about Money with Your Church?

Let me close with one final implication of Paul's example. Given how many opportunities there are to pastor your church when talking about money, why would you not entrust this to a pastor?

When presenting the monthly financial report, encouraging the congregation to give, and discussing the church's financial needs, don't just communicate the financial details. Instead, like Paul, put finances into the context of larger matters, like faith in God's providence and his eternal rewards. Whenever you talk about money, seek to pastor your church.

ABOUT THE AUTHOR

Jamie Dunlop is an associate pastor of Capitol Hill Baptist Church in Washington, D. C. He is the author of Budgeting for a Healthy Church: Aligning Finances with Biblical Priorities for Ministry.

Handling Your Church's Finances with Transparency and Integrity

Jenny Terry

How we spend money reveals what we value. Jesus tells us:

> Do not store up for yourselves treasures on earth, where moths and vermin destroy, and where thieves break in and steal. But store up for yourselves treasures in heaven, where moths and vermin do not destroy and where thieves do not break in and steal. *For where your treasure is, there your heart will be also. (Matt. 6:19–21)*

How churches spend the money entrusted to them should matter greatly to believers. And yet, we find ourselves living in a world where it's hard to talk about money. We get squeamish when the topic of money comes up. Should it be the same way in the church?

Jesus didn't shy away from talking about money. In fact, we see in the Gospels that of his thirty-nine parables, eleven of them talk about money.

How should this shape the way we think and talk about how the church spends the Lord's money?

Several years ago, I found myself handling finances and administration for a rapidly growing church with multiple campuses. During that time, I saw the pastors take on a private posture when handling the church's finances. There was no transparency, which meant there was no accountability. Even between staff and lay elders, there was a tremendous lack of transparency regarding how church finances were being handled and how money was being spent. Unfortunately, this led to ballooning operating expenses that regularly outpaced the church's giving. We were consistently operating in the red. To make matters worse, there were obvious areas where we could and should have pulled back spending.

Again, how we spend money reveals what we value.

Pastors often caution their church members about the dangers of money. But pastors themselves aren't immune. When Jesus warns us about our hearts and our treasures, he's not condemning money in and of itself, but rather the greediness that so easily grabs our hearts and convinces us money is all we need.

Church members tithe their hard-earned money; they give sacrificially, trusting those in charge that their gifts will be stewarded to serve God's kingdom. When we give, we're not just investing our money; we're investing our allegiance. And we're trusting that the elders in charge of stewarding the church's finances are doing so with the utmost integrity.

Jesus is the perfect example of a man of integrity. He is faultless, sincere, righteous, and without blemish. We are called to be imitators of Christ in all we do (Eph. 5:1). That includes modeling his integrity in our handling of money.

To that end, here are three basic principles that I'm convinced lead to a healthy financial culture, especially in a local church.

1. LEAN INTO TRANSPARENCY

Churches should lean into transparency about how money is allocated *and* spent. A church should be transparent not only about its intentions but its actions. In other words, yes, the budget should be visible to church members. But also should a regularly updated report that offers a snapshot of recent spending and giving. These practices create accountability. Sometimes, there may be a thoughtful reason for not sharing a specific detail; but generally speaking, make as much information available as possible. Transparency is a core building block of trust; it communicates that leaders are committed to faithfully stewarding the church's resources—not merely saying that intend to.

This kind of transparency invites everyone to observe how God is advancing his kingdom through faithful giving of your fellow church members. It reminds us that giving is meant to lead to worship. Just as we teach our members how to pray by praying together on Sunday mornings, we also teach our members how to view their money by faithfully spending the resources entrusted to the church.

When money is handled properly, those handling the finances should count it a joy and privilege to share the details of what the church is doing with spending their money. It's an incredible opportunity to paint a picture for the entire congregation of how God is using their sacrificial giving in both big and small ways.

A Litmus Test of Transparency

For pastors who are committed to building a healthy financial culture, administer a quick litmus test by asking how much your current staff feels they can share about how the church's money is spent. Do they feel like there are things they need to hide in order to protect the image of one or more of the pastors? If so, that is dangerously problematic.

Trust starts with transparency. Transparency enables accountability.

2. INVITE ACCOUNTABILITY

Church leaders should share details about the church's budget, and then create opportunities for members to ask questions. This goes a long way in building a healthy financial culture.

Why? First of all, because it forces church leaders to remain humble. A church member might ask a question that reveals areas in the budget that could use prayerful reconsideration. When church leaders are open to adjusting something as important as how the church spends money, it provides a powerful example of the body of Christ working together.

When spending is not treated with integrity, church leaders will be tempted to get defensive when members start to ask questions. I saw this happen firsthand. When members' questions started to reveal too much about the wayward spending of the church, they were accused of lacking trust and faith in their leaders.

What a shame. Elders should gladly welcome questions about the budget as an additional layer of accountability that protects their own hearts from the pitfalls of greed.

Lastly, inviting accountability sets the stage to develop internal controls for checks and balances. Putting appropriate safeguards in place gives peace of mind that those handling the church's finances are guided by integrity.

3. Commit to moderation.

In the summer of 2012, the church where I handled finances and administration had undertaken a $2 million dollar construction and renovation project. We were highly leveraged, and week over week, more and more money was going out to pay for both expected and unexpected expenses associated with the project.

At one point, the senior pastor told me not to worry about our burgeoning expenses, that I should rest like a Calvinist, knowing God is in control.

Quite right, God is in control. And yet, we are not passive bystanders to the work God is doing in and around us. It's not mere coincidence that Jesus spent so much time talking about money. He knew that money makes an alluring ruler that tries to convince us it's more valuable than the greatest gift we've been given: eternal life through Jesus Christ.

In the years since that exchange, I've reflected a lot on why it was so unsettling. In the end, I've come to see that even the best intentions can be clouded when we allow our love of money, power, and image to overshadow our love for God. When money takes hold of our hearts, we are tempted to dismiss the stronghold it has over us, and we convince ourselves that our worldly desires are somehow righteous. After all, the excessive spending habits I saw firsthand were touted as if they were *for* the advancement of the kingdom.

How much more powerful it would have been if the senior pastor had committed to pulling back spending, working together with my team and the board of elders to cut costs, rather than defaulting to another sermon series on money and giving. Maybe we didn't actually *need* to spend a quarter of a million dollars on a state-of–the-art speaker system. Perhaps the $75,000 system would have worked just fine. Maybe we didn't *need* to spend $50,000 a year on coffee and coffee equipment to prove we were a "hospitable" church. Perhaps we just needed to define hospitality biblically.

Of course, this example is not meant to suggest that we should question every decision made by elders who have proven themselves to be trustworthy. Those of us working in a diaconal capacity need to prayerfully balance asking questions with our call to submit to faithful elder leadership. The point here is that elders and deacons can commit to moderation, and both have a role to play in committing the church's resources.

As a general principle, I'd encourage churches to commit to moderation when it comes to how we spend money. We simply cannot properly value the kingdom of God and at the same time be driven by self-centered, thing-oriented spending.

CONCLUSION

How we spend money reveals what we value. And I pray your church's spending reveals that your greatest treasure is Christ himself and his gift of forgiving, transforming grace.

ABOUT THE AUTHOR

Jenny Terry currently works as the Director of Business Operations for Buffer and serves on multiple boards in the Fintech and SaaS space. She currently lives in Louisville, KY with her husband and daughter where she is a member at Third Avenue Baptist Church.

Who Should Know How Much Everyone Makes?

Jason Read

Pay transparency is a growing trend in the business world. Want to know how much each employee at social media giant Buffer makes? You can look it up on their website. Similarly, Whole Foods publishes the average salary for every position. Norway's government recently took it a step further. They made each Norwegian citizen's salary available via an online searchable database. But be forewarned, people can see a log of who looked them up!

Some states in the U.S. have legislated a measure of pay transparency. For example, South Carolina's Act to Establish Pay Equity makes it illegal for employers to prohibit their employees from sharing wage information. Colorado's Equal Pay for Equal Work Act requires employers to include compensation ranges with job postings.

Should churches proactively disclose staff salaries to the members? When a member or employee asks for the information, is it wise to share? Put simply, is pay transparency a good idea for the church?

When considering whether to share salary information with the whole church or one inquisitive member, try to process that question with two goals: build ownership and maintain unity.

GOAL #1: BUILD OWNERSHIP

Budget meetings in the church can span the spectrum from a simple FYI with no voting to accepting amendments from the floor. Some lean toward the simple, highlighting only high-level categories. Others prefer the detailed approach, showing every cent spent on every item.

My goal in our church budget process is to faithfully steward resources by aligning our budget with Christ's stated purpose for the local church, which is to make disciples (Matt. 28:19–20). While our Chief Shepherd certainly does not need our money for his mission, our resources significantly impact the church's work.

When each part of the church body works correctly, the whole body grows up (Eph. 4:16). This means members contribute to one another's lives and have an active role in each other's discipleship. The budget intersects with this culture because it's a commitment to sustaining a gospel ministry. It's a matter of discipleship. It follows that voting on or affirming the budget is part of overseeing each other's discipleship.

But back to the question: how much information does the church need to know in order to own its budget meaningfully? Over the years, I've discovered an inverse relationship between the number of cells in a budget spreadsheet and the average person's ability to understand it. Ownership minus understanding trends toward pie in the sky.

Prudence lies somewhere in the middle space, between only knowing the bottom number and being able to recite every line. When members have a working knowledge without being overwhelmed with details, they will feel greater ownership of the budget and the ministry.

That might mean sharing pay data. It could be helpful to know how much the church is investing in the ministry of the Word compared to other expenses like building maintenance. Both are important, but one is an obvious priority over the other. Members being in the know regarding staff salaries may also help curb pastors being underpaid. If churches understand the correlation between a pastor's salary and the ministry of the Word, they will not underpay him purposefully.

Conversely, combining all salaries into a single line might be sufficient. This strategy can prevent less mature church members from becoming distracted by the specifics. If your church goes this route, I recommend taking the time to teach the congregation the church's salary philosophy. The Lord gives us instructions for paying our pastors (1 Cor 9:1–14; 1 Tim 5:17–18). Members must be obedient and care for those who care for them.

I know of at least one church that lumps the bottom line for salaries but makes individual numbers available on request in the church office. This may be a good middle-ground solution. What should be obvious is that there is not a universal answer to this universal question. Knowing what will best serve each church takes wisdom.

MAINTAIN UNITY

As believers, we're all called to eagerly maintain the unity of the Spirit (Eph 4:1–6). A united church is a spectacular reminder of God's eternal, cosmic plan to unite all things in Christ. Unfortunately, budget meetings and church finance conversations are notoriously divisive. Division, regardless of its cause, harms a church's gospel witness. Budgets should not be a source of division in our congregations. So, let me ask you, church leader, would sharing individual salary data maintain or threaten unity in your church?

I know of too many churches recovering from financial mismanagement or sinful impropriety. Both scenarios erode the trust members have in their leaders. In the wake of a scandal, a bent toward honest transparency is generally the best course. Even apart from scandal, I can imagine other scenarios in which more detail, whether on salaries or utilities, will best serve a congregation. For example, if a church has come into maturity in valuing Word ministry and has worked overtime to compensate their lead pastor fairly, it may be very encouraging to share the information so they may be encouraged in the excellent work they did together!

We should share Solomon's sentiment when he said, "A tranquil heart gives life to the flesh, but envy makes the bones rot" (Pro. 14:30). While not always, envy often lies at the root of many arguments against pay transparency. If employees know how much everyone makes, envy sprouts up in the soil of the team. On the other hand, it may also be a cause for rejoicing that other brothers are being taken care of.

Paul presses on the churches in Galatia and us today when he says, "walk by the Spirit…you will not gratify the desires of the flesh" (Gal. 5:16). Those desires include enmity, jealousy, strife, and dissensions (Gal. 5:19–21). Interestingly, research by organizations like Payscale and WorldatWork suggests that transparency increases employee engagement, job satisfaction, and teamwork. I don't think we should assume that church staff will necessarily choose to gratify their sinful desires. Instead, the Spirit empowers pastors and staff to trust the Lord for their daily bread and celebrate it being given to others as well.

So, is it wise to trust the Spirit and immediately sing salaries from the hilltops? Not necessarily. Having a compensation policy may also be a warranted defense against envy and division. That policy, given to staff and available to anyone, should outline things like a biblical framework for why the staff is paid, the principles for compensation, and an overview of when compensation is evaluated and who is involved in that process. That may be short of publishing pay data, but it goes a long way toward removing the curtain's mystery and ensuring your staff understands the what and the why behind their compensation.

Additionally, I would encourage you to maintain unity by building a culture where it's okay to talk about money in general and compensation in particular. Like every other member, pastors have bills, too. This is not an encouragement to fall in love with money. Elders should be above reproach in this matter (1 Tim 3:2–3). I've often found myself stuck, needing to talk about making more money but also suspicious of my own heart and fearful of being misunderstood. Regardless of your polity or staffing structure and regardless of whether you publish salary data, who is actively making it easier for church staff to talk about their pay?

CONCLUSION

Pay transparency in the church comes with significant risks. Some will be confused by total compensation made up of salary and benefits. Other members may be tempted to compare the pastor's salary to theirs, risking envy and tension. As a pastor, I don't love these conversations. But if sharing my salary helps to maintain unity and gives the church meaningful ownership of the ministry, then I joyfully accept.

Therein lies the challenge of shepherding; we must know our people and their needs. Sometimes, sharing information will build up; sometimes, it will tear down. Rather than hide information out of fear or carelessly publish it on the street corners, aim to shepherd your church toward meaningful membership and unity in Christ.

ABOUT THE AUTHOR

Jason Read is the executive pastor at Heritage Bible Church in Greer, South Carolina.

Preparing Pastors for Retirement

Brad Thayer

A church's health is nurtured by biblically sound preaching. God uses his infallible Word to grow his church. But this isn't an article about preaching; it's about retirement.

The connection between sound preaching and a congregation's health is obvious. But what's the relationship between a church's health and a pastor's retirement? Is there a connection? Not directly. Instead, the connection is indirect by virtue of *pastoral longevity.* A church that is thoughtful about its pastor's retirement contributes to his longevity, and with longevity comes health. The longer a man pastors one church, generally speaking the more fruit the Spirit will produce through his faithful preaching and shepherding (1 Cor. 3:5–11).

A generous compensation package contributes to longevity. Pastors experience their congregation's love when their family "lacks nothing" (Titus 3:13). They're free to "shepherd the flock of God . . . not for shameful gain, but eagerly" (1 Pet. 5:2). If you play a role in setting your pastor's compensation, then this article is primarily for you. Healthy churches can proactively plan for and financially invest in their pastor's retirement as a way to encourage his longevity.

I need to give a qualifier. Retirement benefits are not applicable in all settings. Many pastors are bi-vocational or are in poorer regions. Some serve overseas and depend on limited financial support or they are from countries where retirement is not a thing. Not all churches will handle this subject the same. Though my comments are aimed at American churches, each congregation should be thoughtful in how it cares for its pastor.

PROACTIVELY PLAN FOR YOUR PASTOR'S RETIREMENT

The Lord has numbered every one of our days (Job 4:1–6; Ps. 90:10; Heb. 9:27). None of us should presume upon tomorrow (Jam. 4:13–17). Your pastor may not live to see retirement. Nonetheless, it's prudent to plan for the day when he no longer shepherds his church. That may be due to diminished health or the inability to keep pace with the ministry's daily demands. Therefore, proactively plan for his retirement—his *redeployment* to a new season of ministry.

Here are some suggested ways to plan.

Where opportunities present themselves, encourage him to use his gifts to serve other churches and ministries. If possible, give him the freedom to preach at other churches, teach at seminaries, write for ministries, provide leadership for your denomination or network, go on mission trips, and more. These opportunities expand his relationships and hone his gifts that could be used in a new season of ministry when he retires as your full-time pastor.

Encourage financial planning early in his ministry. For example, direct him to a certified financial planner to help set reasonable goals. Ensure he has a living will. Offer to pay for those services within his first five years. If he's young, he may have student loans and would be helped by Dave Ramsey's *Financial Peace University*. Whatever it may be, have someone come alongside your pastor and his wife to help them plan.

Organize wise counselors to help plan for his retirement. Proverbs 15:22 says, "Without counsel plans fail, but with many advisors they succeed." Your pastor, his family, his fellow elders, and the congregation will be helped by having "many advisors" figuring out a plan for his retirement. Consider creating a "Retirement Oversight Team"[1] comprised of elders, deacons, and trusted members. When your pastor is between the ages of 50–55, this group could work with the pastor and, when necessary, his wife, to answer questions like:

- What's an approximate timeframe for a planned retirement?
- What is the transition plan for his replacement?
- Who are possible replacement candidates?
- Are there ways we'll care for his widow or special-needs children?
- How can we steward his years of wisdom, experience, and relationships into retirement?
- What's the progress of his financial plan?

1 Evangelical Counsel for Financial Accountability, "8 Essentials of Retirement Planning for Ministers and Churches" in the *Church Essentials Series*. (E-book), 22.

Any plan is just that—a plan. They can be changed or scrapped entirely, so don't be anxious. But it could serve many people well to plan early.

FINANCIALLY INVEST IN YOUR PASTOR'S RETIREMENT

The Bible commends compensating pastors for their faithful labor. Paul said, "Let the elders who rule well be considered worthy of double honor, especially those who labor in preaching and teaching. For the Scripture says, 'You shall not muzzle an ox when it treads out the grain,' and, 'The laborer deserves his wages'" (1 Tim. 5:17–18; cf. Gal. 6:6).

Where possible, seek to pay your pastor. Your church is well served by the financial investment made in faithful shepherds.

How much should you pay him? It depends. But lean into generosity and trust, as the word *double* in the passage above suggests.[2] In an American context, it's good to structure his compensation with a "salary and benefits" package

2 Jamie Dunlop, *Budgeting for a Healthy Church: Aligning Finances with Biblical Priorities for Ministry* (Grand Rapids, MI: Zondervan, 2019), 78-84.

versus a "lump-sum" package. The former reduces tax liability and ensures funds are spent appropriately. This also allows a pastor to know how much he and his family have for living expenses and charitable giving. Generally, a good package will be comprised of five parts: salary, housing allowance, healthcare, retirement, and ministry resources and education.

Give generously to all these, including a retirement plan. Any man qualified to pastor is not in ministry for the money (1 Tim. 3:3; Titus 1:7). If you cannot trust him with money, he should not be your pastor! More lucrative careers are in the private sector; he may have even left one to be your pastor. The standard expectation is 80–90% of pre-retirement income during retirement. Your pastor is probably aware of his financial limitations to meet that expectation. He's faithfully providing for his family, giving generously to the church, and saving for emergencies, but not much is left over. So give generously to his retirement.

If possible, contribute 10% of his salary to a retirement plan. If he begins pastoring young like I did, those funds will grow with salary increases and investment earnings. Other factors may necessitate giving more than 10%. If you're providing church-owned housing, he may need additional income to buy or rent when he retires. He may have special-needs children that will be financially dependent on him. These factors may warrant a 15–20% retirement contribution.

Another factor to consider is living expenses during different seasons of life. Pay scales trend upward with tenure, but so do costs with a growing family. (Trust me! I have three teenage girls and a tween boy.) So the peak earning years when a pastor may be able to invest in his retirement are limited. If he does—and lovingly encourage him to do so—matching contributions are a helpful incentive. For example, give a 10% base contribution and then match his contributions to a certain percentage.

I'm no financial planner. I'm a pastor, so consult with someone knowledgeable of a pastor's unique tax status and investment options before making retirement contributions. But one retirement plan exclusively designed for ministries is a 403(b). It maximizes the benefits available to pastors: Their contributions are tax-sheltered and not subject to SECA; they can be designated as housing allowance at retirement, and more.

Last bit of advice: Housing and healthcare are the most significant expenses in retirement. If your pastor has opted out of Social Security, that income and Medicare won't be available from his church salary when he retires. It's wise to help him plan for healthcare expenses by redirecting SECA reimbursements to his retirement instead of additional income.

Others may have more creative financial solutions for your pastor's retirement. Great! My encouragement is, if possible, generously invest in it.

A WORD TO PASTORS

Brother pastor, thank you for your service. It may be inconceivable to think about retirement. Right now, you're preparing for the next elders' meeting, or counseling session, or sermon in Isaiah. Those responsibilities matter exponentially more than retirement. Persevere! Labor diligently for the good of the souls entrusted to your care for whom you'll give an account (Heb. 13:17).

Praise God if you've been helped in any way by this advice! Find a trusted leader to figure out how to take steps toward implementation. Continue to devote yourself to the ministry of the Word and prayer. Pray for humility. Seeking counsel requires transparency about your financial management. Be humble to receive advice and correction if necessary.

Lord willing, your church will exist after you're gone. So invest in "faithful men, who will be able to teach others also" (2 Tim. 2:2). Share the pulpit and leadership responsibilities with godly and gifted brothers. You can run longer and faster in ministry with their help. If you're the primary preaching pastor, the burden is on you to create a culture where members aren't solely dependent upon you for teaching and shepherding. They will be better prepared for the day you retire after years of being taught and cared for by a plurality of elders.

CONCLUSION

Having pastored the same church for fourteen years, I know the fruit born from longevity. Our relationship of unity, love, and trust wasn't forged overnight; it came through endurance and generosity. These saints have been patient with my shortcomings and generous with their love in word and in deed. We've grown together through long-suffering and longevity which will, Lord willing, continue until either my retirement or our Savior's return.

ABOUT THE AUTHOR

Brad Thayer is an associate pastor/administration of Mount Vernon Baptist Church in Sandy Springs, Georgia.

How Much Should We Pay Our Staff

Jamie Dunlop

One factor to consider when deciding how many staff your church should hire is the simple math of how much you pay them. Should you aim at lower compensation so you can hire more staff? What are the spiritual consequences of overpaying or underpaying your staff? Let me suggest two principles to guide your philosophy of staff compensation.

GENEROSITY

Every time the New Testament addresses financial support of church staff and missionaries, it underscores generosity.

- "The one who receives instruction in the word should share *all good things* with their instructor" (Gal. 6:6, emphasis mine).
- "The elders who direct the affairs of the church well are *worthy of double honor*, especially those whose work is preaching and teaching" (1 Tim. 5:17, emphasis mine).
- "Do your best to speed Zenas the lawyer and Apollos on their way; *see that they lack nothing*" (Titus 3:13 ESV, emphasis mine).
- "Please send them on their way in a *manner that honors God*" (3 John 6, emphasis mine).

Don't be stingy with your staff compensation. What benefit is it to you for your pastor to be distracted from ministry because of financial needs? It is possible to be overly generous as well. Extravagant pay is poor stewardship and may warp a pastor's motivations for ministry. After all, he is to be one who is "not pursuing dishonest gain, but eager to serve" (1 Pet. 5:2).

So what constitutes pay that is generous but not extravagant? As with beauty, it would seem that "generous" is in the eye of the beholder. As such, Paul's exhortation in Titus 3:13 is a good summary of appropriate pay: "See that they lack nothing" (ESV). You shouldn't try to provide your staff with everything they could ever wish for. But you want to provide enough that a pastor or staff member is not distracted from ministry because of financial concerns.

How can you be sure your staff are lacking nothing in this regard? I recommend five different data points that can guide your compensation decisions.

First, consider *nonchurch benchmarks.*

How are comparable public servants paid? Similar to pastors, many public officials have agreed to work for less money than they could make on the open market. Yet like a church, their employers don't want them eventually forced into the private sector for want of money. You might find a useful comparison by looking at the compensation package of a local school principal or police chief, or the government pay scale.

You may also want to look at *church benchmarks.* How do other churches pay their staff? Several organizations will sell you benchmarking information for church staff positions in your area. Of course, churches are generally not known for being generous with their compensation. Don't assume that all or even most churches in your benchmarking set are being faithful in paying their staff. Rather than buying benchmarking data, you might find it more useful to exchange compensation information with a few churches in your area that you trust in this regard.

Consider what *replacement cost* would be for this position. If a staff member were to leave, would you need to increase (or be able to decrease) the size of the compensation package in order to attract an individual who would do the job equally well? Then you are probably not paying what the work is worth and should consider revising what you are paying them.

Fourth, look through a *sample personal budget*. What makes for a sustainable family budget at different stages of life in your locality? Ask this question of several people in their fifties and sixties, as those much younger may not fully understand what it really costs to raise a family, and those who are older may no longer remember. Why do this if you are paying your staff based on their work rather than on their needs? Because compensation is not a purely deductive process and you should check what you think the work is worth against a typical level of need.[1]

Finally, have some *honest conversations*. Ensure that someone in leadership in your church speaks regularly with your staff about how their compensation package is serving them and their families. Do they feel there is parity across staff? Are they finding their ministry hampered for want of money? Consider that feedback carefully.

That short phrase in Titus 3 is remarkably powerful in summarizing these goals for compensation. "See that they lack nothing." Paying your pastor is one of the most important things your church budget can do. As such, unless your congregation really doesn't have the money, one of your top budget priorities should be to pay a pastor and to ensure that his compensation is a help to his ministry, erring on the side of generosity.

1 Three notes regarding compensation: (1) Do not assume that just because a compensation package worked for a person's predecessor it will work for them as well. Different people have different needs (say, particular health issues or family they need to care for in a different country). (2) Some churches start with a benchmark and then subtract what a staff member would have given to the church, surmising that it's more tax-efficient to not pay them this in the first place. Don't do this! Since giving is one of the main purposes for income (Eph. 4:28) and pastors are to be examples to the flock (1 Pet. 5:3), don't deprive pastors of the joy of giving simply because they work for a church. (3) Even if your pastor is single, it is wise to consider needs based on the needs of a family. After all, he may one day have a family, or even if he doesn't, his replacement might. Don't pay less merely because of the marital status of your pastor.

HOW MUCH TO PAY ADMINISTRATIVE STAFF

I find it interesting that Paul's rationale to pay pastors in 1 Timothy 5:18 is not grounded in their office but their work: "The laborer deserves his wages." As such, this principle offers rationale for paying administrative staff as well as a pastor. It implies that you should pay them what their work is worth, not how much you think they need.

But shouldn't people working for a church make less money? No. If the laborer deserves his wages, he deserves what his work is worth. Evaluating what his work is "worth" might be complicated for a pastoral position, but it is comparatively straightforward for an administrative position.

Since administrative jobs are often similar to positions in other nonprofit organizations and businesses in your area, you might find that regional compensation surveys conducted by the government are a good guide. Some struggling churches might not be able to pay market rate for a time. But over the long term, adjust your staff size to fit the available budget.

TRUST

In addition to generosity, consider the importance of *trust.* Several years before I began working as a pastor at my church, I served on our church's compensation committee. I did this while working in a career in business, having no idea that the salary I was helping to set would one day be my own. I'm in the unique position of having designed a church compensation plan that I now live with! One lesson I've learned from that transition—from layman to staff pastor—is the inherent vulnerability of working for a church.

Consider, by way of analogy, the difference between working for a large corporation and working for your father's small business. Both situations involve trust—but trust in a family-run company is different because *the relationship extends beyond the business.*

When I worked in the business world, my employer expected me to look out for myself, and I negotiated my compensation with that in mind. When I began to work for my church, however, the dynamic shifted. It was more like working for the family business. Of course, we discussed my compensation before I accepted the job, but not in the freewheeling way that's expected in the for-profit world. The implicit agreement, now that I work for my church, is that I will spend my energy for them—and that they will care for me. When that vulnerability is held in trust, it makes for a wonderful working relationship between a pastor and his church.

As a church, hold that trust carefully. One way you can do that if you *don't* work for a church is by understanding how your church's pay package works. Do you know the tax burdens and benefits of working as a pastor? Do you know how much your pastor's pay has increased in the last five years relative to inflation? Do you know how your church accounts for your pastor's housing (which in the US has special tax treatment)? How confident are you that staff are paid in parity with each other, accounting for merit, experience, and education? If your general response is, "those details aren't of interest to me," or "it's my pastor's job to bring up any problems with compensation," I would challenge you as to whether you fully appreciate the vulnerable place that your church staff are in.

WHAT ABOUT STAFF IN FINANCIAL DISTRESS

What should a church do when its own staff are struggling financially? It is important in these situations to keep in mind the principle I outlined earlier from 1 Timothy 5, that it is a person's labor that makes them worthy of pay. Here are some questions to ask when your staff are in financial hardship:

1. Is This Our Fault?

Has the church been underpaying for the work they receive? In that case, the church might provide a bonus to remedy this wrong in addition to adjusting compensation. A staff member's level of need is not irrelevant to this assignment: only in unusual situations (as with a trainee) should a church hire a staff member *knowing* that compensation will not be sufficient to meet their needs.

2. Are They in the Wrong Job?

You should not increase compensation simply because a person's needs have increased. It may be that this person's needs are simply more than this job can support. In that case you might help them upskill so they can make a transition to a different job.

3. *Are Finances Being Mismanaged?*

Perhaps financial distress has come because a staff member doesn't manage their money well. This may be cause for (1) questioning whether a pastor is disqualified from office by failing to "manage his own household well" (1 Tim. 3:4 ESV); and/ or (2) teaching them about financial management.

4. *Do They Need Temporary Financial Help?*

If they do, then assist them in a way that does not compromise their dignity or respect. Do be sure, however, to make it clear that this is benevolence and not compensation, as to not confuse Jesus's principle that the worker is worthy of their wages.[2] As is true with any use of benevolence funds, this is a good short-term solution but not a viable long-term solution.

2 A separation between benevolence and compensation is important in your communication to them, but the two may be indecipherable for tax reasons. Most likely, benevolence to a staff member will be seen by taxing authorities as taxable income.

EDITOR'S NOTE

This article is adapted from *Budgeting for a Healthy Church: Aligning Finances with Biblical Priorities for Ministry* by Jamie Dunlop, ©2019. Used by permission of Zondervan.

ABOUT THE AUTHOR

Jamie Dunlop is an associate pastor of Capitol Hill Baptist Church in Washington, D. C. He is the author of Budgeting for a Healthy Church: Aligning Finances with Biblical Priorities for Ministry.

Addressing Staff Salary Discrepancies

Dennis Blythe

The personnel committee of First Church sits down for its annual staff salary review. After a few moments of silently perusing the numbers, someone eventually verbalizes what everyone else is thinking: "Why is Pastor Brian paid so much less than Pastor Larry? Hasn't Brian been here longer? And Larry hasn't even finished seminary. That doesn't seem right."

Second Church, across town, has a different question. Word on the ministerial street is that every other church in the community pays better than they do. And when they recently had an open role to fill they were discouraged to learn their leading candidate declined taking a position elsewhere. The pastor couldn't help but wonder, "Was it because of the money?"

These are fair questions, and in some cases, they may have good answers. But unfortunately, for many churches, there is often no rhyme or reason for why staff salaries are what they are. For some churches, the issues could be attributed to a change in leadership or a new philosophy of staff compensation. In another instance, it might be that the church got off track due to some lean years financially. And then there's the real possibility that leaders simply made a few unwise or uninformed decisions.

So, what do we do when there seems to be a discrepancy (perhaps more than one) in our staff salary structure?

GUIDING PRINCIPLES

There are three guiding principles church leaders should bear in mind as they work to address these issues.

1. It's essential to sit down with church leaders and develop a plan.

Identify where the discrepancies are; determine an order of priority for addressing them (begin with your most valued roles/individuals first); and then prayerfully take steps in your annual budget planning to ensure that staff members are compensated appropriately.

2. Create a staff salary structure that you can evaluate and use for the future.

Begin by putting on paper what the actual salary range for each category on your staff is currently (i.e. pastors, directors, associates, administrative assistants). Then, using reliable salary survey data, local salary comparisons, and demographics of the church and community, determine what your target range needs to be for each category. For a variety of reasons, this will look different from church to church.

The low end of the range for a category should represent what a starting salary would be before any unique factors are applied. The high end of the range should represent what the church would be able/willing to pay a highly qualified and experienced individual in that category. It's important to note that this tool should be reviewed and updated annually. A starting salary of $50,000 shouldn't still be $50,000 three years from now. The pay ranges need to increase as salaries change in order to account for inflation.

Questions you might ask as you develop a salary structure for your church include: Are we fair in our compensation? Are we consistent? Are we competitive? Is this sustainable?

3. Establish consistent criteria for setting and evaluating salaries.

One reason churches get out of balance with their compensation structure is they will sometimes set a salary without considering the bigger picture. A common mistake is to think, "We just need to pay them whatever it's going to take to get them here." In some cases, that may mean the number is lower than it should be. In other cases, it is higher than it should be. More often than not, however, this approach will leave you with a bit of a mess and eventual discrepancies and inconsistencies. As you establish your salary criteria, it's important to consider both the *role* and the *individual*.

SALARIES FOR DIFFERENT ROLES

There are at least five questions to ask when setting a salary for a particular *role*.

1. What's the scope of responsibility?

In most cases, the greater the responsibility, the higher the salary. Variables might include supervision responsibilities (of both staff and volunteers), the extent of financial oversight, decision-making authority, etc. This is a common reason that two seemingly similar pastoral roles might be paid differently.

2. What's the geographic location of the church?

Because cost of living varies across the country, a church in a major city on the West Coast is understandably going to pay differently than a rural church in the Midwest.

3. What are the demographics of the church?

As an example, if a church located in an upper-middle class suburb is made up largely of white-collar professionals, that ought to inform, to a degree, how they compensate members of the staff.

4. What are other churches paying for this role?

It's not about keeping up with the Joneses, but it's important to be comparable and competitive with your pay, whenever possible. Networking and exchanging information with other churches may help you know if you are low, high, or right on target. To the extent possible, be sure you are comparing apples to apples.

5. What's the church's overall budget?

To be clear, a big budget shouldn't necessarily mean big salaries, nor should a small budget necessarily mean small salaries. There are small churches who pay handsomely, and there are larger churches who are somewhat stingy. With that said, it's important for a church to live within its means. Sometimes discrepancy issues arise because a church has stretched itself too thin and is trying to employ more staff than it can afford. A hard but sometimes necessary decision is to operate with fewer staff so that a church can adequately compensate those it has.

DETERMINING SALARIES FOR INDIVIDUALS

Additionally, there are four considerations to keep in mind when setting a salary for a specific *individual.*

1. What's the individual's value to the church?

While it's true that no staff member is indispensable or irreplaceable, there are individuals who bring unique value to the table for a church. It may be their skillset, institutional knowledge, or something more intangible. Within reason, it's certainly appropriate for such persons to be compensated accordingly.

2. How long has this person served on staff at the church?

If someone has been with you for a long time, it stands to reason they have served well (or they wouldn't still be there). It makes sense for them to earn more than the employee who is just starting out.

3. How long has this person served in vocational ministry?

This is primarily for those serving in a ministerial or pastoral role and may have come from another church. A seasoned leader with 20-plus years of vocational service under his belt will likely be paid more than someone in a similar role who is serving in his first church staff job.

4. What about education?

Each church will uniquely set any education prerequisites it may have for specific staff roles. The time and effort invested in preparation and training ought to count for something in the consideration of their pay, similarly to one's years of experience.

ADDITIONAL PRINCIPLES

Here are some additional principles to keep in mind when addressing discrepancy issues:

- Be consistent with how you pay similar roles on your staff. In other words, be careful about doing for one what you don't do for another. An example of this might be, "We are paying Mary a higher wage, but since the budget is tight, we'll hire Linda for a little less and just give her more vacation instead."
- Neither gender, marital status, nor family status should be criteria for one's salary. Churches can find themselves on a slippery slope if they decide to pay one candidate more than another simply because one is married and the other is not. Likewise, the staff member who has five children shouldn't be compensated more than the one who doesn't have children simply because their family has more dependent-related expenses.
- Consider rewarding short-term or one-time exceptional performances with a bonus, as opposed to a permanent pay increase. A couple of "good job" raises that are permanent can quickly create the beginning of a discrepancy.
- On the other hand, use a salary adjustment (or merit raise) to reward a demonstrated increase in value to the church over an extended period of time. Don't misunderstand—there is certainly a place for permanent increases to one's pay, but if not administered wisely, they can quickly stretch your salary structure. (Note: this is different than a cost-of-living adjustment the church might provide staff-wide on a more regular basis.)

CONCLUSION

Finally, it is important for church leaders to recognize that addressing salary discrepancies likely won't happen, in full, in a single budget year. For many churches, it may take several years, but it is important to stay the course. The matter of compensating your church staff fairly (and even generously) is not an unspiritual one. In fact, it's biblical and God-glorifying, and churches should work diligently toward making it a reality.

ABOUT THE AUTHOR

Dennis Blythe is the executive pastor of The Church at Brook Hills in Birmingham, Alabama.

Advocating for Your Own Pay

Jamie Dunlop

When is it appropriate for a pastor to advocate for changes in his own compensation? If a pastor is "not a lover of money" (1 Tim. 3:3), shouldn't he take whatever the church gives him without complaining? I believe a pastor should take an active role in making sure his pay package is adequate. But there are a few things to keep in mind when you (pastors) do this.

Be careful that you don't mislead your church as to how much you cost. Assume your church *wants* to see that you "lack nothing." Help them do their job! Imagine you're getting ready to pastor a church. You take the job even though the pay seems low. You think to yourself, "I can make this work for now, and I'm sure we can adjust things later."

But you don't make that clear when you are hired. Now, three years in, you find you need to take a second job to make ends meet, and you resent the church for not taking better care of you (which may be a valid concern). But remember: you accepted the job without complaint—and you're only now telling them that you need more money, and that you've *always* known you'll need more money. Do you see how they might feel misled?

Another factor to keep in mind if you're the main preaching pastor is that your pay package will be the basis for compensating any future staff. For their sakes, help your church come to an appropriately generous compensation philosophy. The reality is that someday you'll need to be replaced, so don't get your church accustomed to unrealistic expectations in how much they need to pay a pastor. If they pay you more than you need, just quietly give it back!

How then should you talk about your own pay? Not in the context of negotiation, but in the context of trust, with the purpose of providing accurate information. You might say something like this: "To be honest, that figure isn't going to work for my family in the long term. For the next year or so, my wife can get a job and we will gladly make this work. But if I'm going to be here long term, which I'd really like, we'll eventually need to move toward a figure more like $XX,XXX. Otherwise, you'll need to find a less expensive pastor."

Be sure to consider any additional factors that might influence your compensation, like experience or the size of the church. Keep in mind that if you're young and inexperienced, you probably don't deserve the pay package your predecessor had. Here are four suggestions for talking with your church about your compensation:

1. *Keep the conversation private.* Ideally, this conversation is between you and a designated leader in your church—perhaps the chair of your compensation committee or the chair of your session. More generally, it's wise for the church to have one lay leader as the point person on all matters of compensation (ideally a non-staff pastor/elder). This way, one person in authority will accept full responsibility for these issues without holding any personal bias.

2. *Your goal is to provide information, not to negotiate.* Unless you're really at the point where finances might force you out of the job, don't pretend that they'll lose you if they don't boost your pay.
3. *Assume they want what you want.* Many churches desire to pay their pastors generously, in line with Scriptural admonitions. Before you accuse them of being too stingy, ask them about their objectives for your compensation. You may be surprised to discover that you're all working for the same goal, even if there is disagreement on how to get there.
4. *Don't make them do all the work.* Work through your personal budget, complete with ministerial tax implications, and humbly ask for their feedback on your expectations and lifestyle.

PAY PRINCIPLES TO AGREE ON

The group that sets pastoral pay should agree on which compensation principles the church should be committed to. Which items in this list can/should you agree to?

- We will pay pastors such that they can support a family on this income alone.
- We will pay pastors such that they can afford to live near where our church meets.
- We will pay pastors such that they can save for retirement (if this isn't already included in the compensation benchmarks you use).
- We will pay pastors enough that they can give money away.
- We will base a pastor's total comp package on one or more suitable external benchmarks.
- We will err on the side of being generous.

CONCLUSION: MAKING VULNERABILITY SAFE

What's the goal in setting staff pay? The goal is to make the vulnerable relationship between a church and its staff feel safe for your staff. You want to ensure their ministry is not hampered by financial concerns. And you want to equip your congregation for works of service. In all this, staff are a means to an end: God-glorifying ministry in the church.

EDITOR'S NOTE

This article is taken from *Budgeting for a Healthy Church: Aligning Finances with Biblical Priorities for Ministry* by Jamie Dunlop, ©2019. Used by permission of Zondervan.

ABOUT THE AUTHOR

Jamie Dunlop is an associate pastor of Capitol Hill Baptist Church in Washington, D. C. He is the author of Budgeting for a Healthy Church: Aligning Finances with Biblical Priorities for Ministry.

Policies

PRINCIPLES FOR A BENEVOLENCE POLICY THAT IS BOTH MERCIFUL AND WISE

Philip Duncanson

To be a Christian is to acknowledge that you are needy. It's one of the marks we read about in the Sermon on the Mount: "Blessed are the poor in spirit for theirs is the kingdom of heaven" (Matt. 5:3). To follow Jesus, you must acknowledge you are spiritually bankrupt and incapable of saving yourself.

A church, then, is a gathering of needy people. Every member recognizes his or her need for the righteousness of Christ (Rom. 3:20), for God's grace (Eph. 2:5), and for forgiveness (Col. 1:13-14).

That said, our physical needs will vary. We may be on the same sea, but we're not in the same boat. Some of our boats have holes, some lack paddles. A church's benevolence ministry begins here: showing each other mercy amidst our different physical needs.

In other words, benevolence is not only about giving people money to help solve their problems. It's about showing others the mercy and love we've been shown. This understanding will both guard against a "savior complex" and keep us from trampling upon one another's God-given dignity.

Here are several principles to keep in mind as you begin to develop your own policy.

FIVE SUGGESTIONS

1. Designate a deacon or a deacon team.

Some churches charge a particular deacon with overseeing benevolence. Capitol Hill Baptist, for instance, names a deacon of member care. My own church distributes that responsibility to all the deacons. Since they are broadly aware of the needs and resources within the body, we feel they are best equipped to minister and discern the best way to approach each situation. A church can ask a non-deacon to be responsible for any given case of benevolence. Yet make sure anyone taking responsibility for these tasks meets the criteria of "the seven" in Acts 6 and of deacons in 1 Timothy 3. Plus, the process will be served by having a consistent individual or team who knows the policies and procedures giving oversight.

2. Budget for benevolence—or at least have a fund.

Some churches have benevolence funds for designated gifts, or they take special offerings. Since our church has frequent benevolence needs, we include a line for benevolence in the annual budget. The deacons oversee that budget item and are empowered to make decisions on how those funds are dispersed. For larger benevolence needs that go beyond what's budgeted, they consult with the elders.

3. Build a culture of vulnerability that will help with communication.

Churches should continually remind members that a benevolence fund exists and what the process is for getting help. But communication goes both ways. Members must communicate their needs, too.

As such, we need a culture of vulnerability where we share the understanding that we're all needy in some way. Hopefully, this will help people ask for help when they should and protect them from suffering silently. This also means the deacons should know how to engage the body, build relationships, and generally be accessible and approachable.

4. Evaluate each situation on its own merits.

Every benevolence request must be evaluated carefully. Financial assistance may not be the answer. Our deacons ask people to fill out an application, which they follow up with a personal consultation, before determining how to best help the individual or family asking for assistance.

The application forces the individual or family to boil down their needs and requests. The consultation allows the team to consider what services and resources in the body might provide solutions without the use of finances. For example, if an individual needs help with dental work, perhaps a dentist in the congregation might help.

The consultation also provides an opportunity to ask questions about overall budgeting patterns or other outside sources of help. Are there foolish expenditures that contribute to the present need, which might solve the problem? Is there a Christian family member who should help instead, lest the church, by taking over the responsibility, tempt that family member to sin (see 1 Tim. 5:8)? These conversations can be uncomfortable, but they're necessary and loving for the sake of the long run. No doubt, they often require some measure of pastoral skill, which is why your deacons should be people "full of the Spirit and wisdom" (Acts 6:3).

5. For long-term benevolence situations, prioritize discipleship.

Some requests are for one-time assistance. Maybe a family has found itself in a financial bind and needs a life jacket. The ask is clear and specific, and a financial gift will quickly solve the problem. However, many benevolence situations require more time and on-going assistance. These provide an opportunity for an on-going discipleship relationship.

Some people haven't been taught how to think about money from a biblical perspective. Therefore, it's helpful to build into benevolence policies things like financial literacy classes, budget development, Scripture memorization, and other practical tools. Each case is different, but in some instances using those tools as prerequisites for on-going assistance can help.

6. If possible, pay merchants directly.

This procedure will help to ensure the money is used directly to fund the need as well as help the ministry keep good financial records. This may come across as a lack of trust, but ultimately you want to be above reproach, creating an environment that leaves no provision for the flesh (Rom. 13:14).

7. Accountability for the deacons?

In order to care for the deacon(s) managing the benevolence policy, it is crucial to have a financial accountability structure in place. The deacon(s) as they make distribution decisions should do so under the oversight of an elder. Check-ins and updates about benevolence cases in the congregation should be regularly shared with the elders.

WHAT ABOUT NON-MEMBERS?

What about helping those who are not members of our church?

Many individuals regard churches as places to go for help. If your church building is located in an area with a lot of walking traffic, I'm sure you inevitably get strangers requesting help. We should thank the Lord for this, but it can also be quite overwhelming.

Here are some principles to keep in mind for those circumstances.

1. If possible, resist handing out cash.

Rather than cash, keep gift cards to restaurants or mass transit cards on hand, as well as non-perishable food items, hygiene kits, and clothes. You want to be able to hand people *something*, but avoid actual cash if you can.

2. Determine a designated one-time amount you're willing to give to strangers.

This is helpful if someone needs rides, shelter, or assistance with a utility. If their request falls within your limit, no extra steps are required. You can provide immediate relief. Just be sure to pay the merchant directly rather than giving the money to the person needing help.

3. Keep an updated list of resources in the area.

Some people will need more assistance than you can provide. So have on hand a list of trusted local shelters, food banks, and other services that you can point people to.

4. Error on the side of mercy.

After dealing with a number of benevolence cases, it's easy to become jaded and even skeptical of every request. Be wise and discerning, but also remember that if you have never been taken advantage of, then perhaps you're not being as merciful or generous as you ought to be.

5. Share the gospel and invite them to church.

I love Peter's example in Acts 3 when he and John come upon the lame beggar at the Beautiful Gate. After the man asks them for money, Peter responds, *"I have no silver and gold, but what I do have I give to you. In the name of Jesus Christ of Nazareth, rise up and walk!"* (Acts 3:6). We may not always have something to give, but we can always give people Jesus.

And that's the goal. You want to have a benevolence policy that seeks to show people the love and mercy of Christ. For he is the one who meets all of our needs.

ABOUT THE AUTHOR

Philip Duncanson is an executive pastor of East Point Church in East Point, Georgia.

Why a Church Constitution Is More Than a Necessary Evil

Greg Gilbert

There's a set of people for whom things like rules, constitutions, and by-laws are endlessly fascinating, people who salivate at the prospect of being asked to revise or—even better!—write from scratch a set of procedural rules for an organization. There is a set of people like that. And then there are normal people! For most of us, constitutions and by-laws are far from fascinating; they're legal documents, necessary administrative evils at best, and at worst, a kind of desiccated straitjacket that hinders the Spirit and turns what should be Spirit-led churches into hide-bound bureaucratic behemoths.

In my experience, though, the people who are most likely to have that sort of low opinion of rules, constitutions, and the like are people who are *about* to lead something, not people who have actually *led*. They're people who are *going to* plant a church or take a pastorate but haven't yet found themselves having to make real decisions in real time in a real congregation. But once you're in a leadership position, it becomes clear pretty fast that solid rules aren't a necessary evil at all;

they're an indispensable weapon for safeguarding the unity of the church.

At the most basic level, rules—whether a constitution or by-laws or governing policies—are just a way of clarifying up-front, for everyone, *who can do what . . . when . . . and under what circumstances.* That's not a minor thing. Get that right, and you'll head off many potentially church-killing arguments and disagreements. Let's explore why that's the case, and why good rules are so important.

FIRST, A CHURCH CONSTITUTION IS A PROFOUNDLY THEOLOGICAL DOCUMENT.

Ultimately, a constitution presents a congregation's way of looking at the Bible's commands about how the church should be structured and organized and then working together to figure out the best and wisest ways to obey those commands. So, the Bible says we're supposed to have a plurality of elders? Great, so how are we supposed to get them? Well, at Third Avenue, for example, we have standing rules that specify that electing an elder requires the recommendation of the elders themselves and then a 75 percent vote of the congregation. That process isn't specified in the Bible. Still, it's our way of trying to obey what *is* specified—the command-by-example to churches to have a plurality of elders who are not hastily appointed and whose authority is recognized by the congregation.

Here's another example: The Bible says that elders are to lead the congregation but that the congregation has final earthly authority (at least in some matters; there is no time now to get into that). So how do you navigate that tension? How do these authorities coincide? At Third Avenue, we've tried to thread that needle in a couple of ways. For most actions like bringing members in, seeing them out, and electing elders and other officers, the elders' recommendation and the church's vote are required. The elders lead, and the congregation executes. There are a couple of actions, however, that the congregation can take without the elders' recommendation *or even over their objection*: They can remove elders from office, and they can amend the constitution (which effectively gives them the right to take back to themselves any authority they have delegated to anyone else). All those authority structures took some thought, creativity, and work, but they're our way of trying to obey the commands and examples we see in the Bible.

SECOND, A GOOD CHURCH CONSTITUTION ALLOWS GOOD-FAITH WINS AND LOSSES.

In my experience, most church fights don't ultimately happen because of an argument's substance. They happen because one party to the argument feels hard-done-by and cheated by the other party. Maybe they lost a key vote at a members' meeting, but the rub comes because they think the meeting wasn't adequately announced or the correct procedure wasn't followed. Clear rules help to cut off, in advance, that feeling. When everyone knows who can do what, when, and under what circumstances, it allows both wins and losses to be accepted in good faith. Most Christians are okay with losing a vote fair and square on mundane matters. It's when they think the vote was illegitimate that gets them riled up.

Thank God, we haven't yet been close to any church-wide disagreement at Third Avenue; the Lord has been kind. In fact, most of the close-run votes happen in our elders' meetings, so we've found it enormously helpful to have a set of by-laws not just for the church as a whole but for the eldership more particularly. Those by-laws have cut the fuse of more than one potential fight.

To give you an example, a few years ago, one of our elders called me before a meeting and asked if I, as chairman, would at some point ask another elder to step out of the room so that the elders could discuss something concerning him. Naturally, I called the brother and asked if he'd be willing to step out, and he said, "No, I think it's important for us to have that conversation all together." Frankly, neither of those guys was being unreasonable; I could see the benefit of both. But we were stuck. Could I, as the chairman, *require* that a duly-elected elder leave the room? Could the board as a whole? Or did that elder have a *right* to be there as someone the church had set aside to be an elder? What if the board wanted to exclude an elder from *every* meeting? Could they do that? You can see the problem! We worked through that specific instance without any real problems, but it was a close-run thing. So, when we adopted by-laws for our elders, we specified a process for asking an elder to leave. It says: "Pursuant to §3.2.9 of the Constitution, the Board may not exclude any Elder from any Meeting of the Board, or any portion thereof, without his consent or the concurrence of three-quarters of the Full Number of Elders." Since we adopted that provision, that problem hasn't come up again. Everyone is fully aware of who can do what, when, and under what circumstances, and it has cut off one line of attack that the enemy could use against our board's unity.

THIRD, A GOOD CHURCH CONSTITUTION CLEARS LOGJAMS AND ENCOURAGES FORWARD PROGRESS.

Imagine a scenario in which the elder board of a new church plant presents to the congregation a budget for the first full fiscal year of the church's existence. Now imagine that even after all the prayers for unity and calls for Christian forbearance, the church votes "no" on the budget. If you don't have any rules, what do you do when the budget fails? Do the elders give it another crack? Does the church elect a budget committee to try again? In the worst-case scenario (but certainly not a far-fetched one), the church could literally be torn apart by not knowing what's supposed to happen next.

A good constitution can prevent that by allowing the church to specify precisely, in advance, what's supposed to happen in the wake of something like a budget failure. I mean, that's essentially what rules are, right? They're the church making some decisions in advance and saying, "Under these circumstances, here's what we want to do. We don't, for example, want to elect an elder unless the other elders recommend that we should." Or, "We don't want to adopt a budget unless this church officer has signed off on it." Or, in the example of the failed budget, "Here's the process we want to follow in the event a budget is voted down." To be sure, that process could take many forms: maybe the church mandates a committee to be elected; maybe it tells the elders that they must try again.

At Third Avenue, for what it's worth, our constitution allows the elders to basically force the budget through by process of attrition! That may seem harsh, but the beauty of it is that when the congregation adopted that constitution provision, they were saying, "Under these circumstances of a failed budget, we don't want our no-vote to logjam the church. We want our elders to listen to us, but finally, we want them to have authority to force it through *so that the church can continue moving forward.*" See the point? Good rules prevent the church from being locked in a months-long struggle over something like that or even breaking apart altogether. They clear the logjam, allow the church to sail on, and do so in a way that enables good faith wins and losses.

ABOVE ALL, A GOOD CONSTITUTION PROTECTS THE UNITY OF THE CHURCH.

I've often thought of our rules at Third Avenue as a kind of "explosion containment unit." They take disagreements and fights that otherwise might spread uncontrolled through a church, dampen them, and channel them into productive places. Here are some of the things our rules have allowed me to say to various members over the years, things that I think have cut off potentially damaging fights within our church:

- "Brother, I understand that you want to nominate Jim to be an elder, but the church has decided in its constitution that it doesn't want elder nominations to come from the floor of a members' meeting. It wants its elders to nominate new elders. Of course, the church can change that rule by amending the constitution if it wants to, but for now, it would be out of order for you to nominate Jim from the floor."

- "Sister, I know you want to have a church-wide conversation about how often we take the Lord's Supper, but the church has specifically asked the elders to have that conversation among themselves and make that decision. Of course, the church can change that decision by amending the constitution, but for now, it's decided it doesn't want to have that conversation as a committee of the whole."
- "Brother elders, I realize that we would unanimously prefer if we could spend this money for a missionary in a closed country without taking a congregational vote on it. But when the church adopted its rules, it reserved for itself the right to vote on certain-sized expenditures that aren't in the budget. Maybe it would be wise to carve out some more exceptions to that rule for the future, but we'll have to do that by asking the church to amend its rules. Until then, we can't make this expenditure without a church vote."
- "Sister, I know you feel like two weeks isn't enough time for you to consider your vote on this pastoral candidate, but in its constitution, the church decided for various reasons that all it wanted was two weeks to consider this question. You can ask them to change that and lengthen the time in the future, but the way to do that will be by offering a constitutional amendment."

I hope you can see what I mean by saying that a constitution is a deeply theological document and a powerful defensive weapon against disunity. Satan is endlessly creative in figuring out ways to fracture churches, and of course, any church's unity is ultimately preserved only by God's grace and power. But at the very least, don't underestimate how much good rules can cut off some of the enemy's most obvious lines of attack—dampening, redirecting, and even preventing some of the fights and disagreements that otherwise would have the potential to destroy the church.

ABOUT THE AUTHOR

Greg Gilbert is the Senior Pastor of Third Avenue Baptist Church in Louisville, Kentucky. You can find him on Twitter at @greggilbert.

How a Lack of Trellis Undermines Ministry

Jonathan Rourke

San Diego is a military county. Camp Pendleton lies to the north of my church, Miramar to the south, and the city itself is the home-port of the Pacific fleet. To say we are influenced by the presence of military personnel is an understatement. These men and women appreciate the need for order, structure, and clear communication. For them it can mean the difference between life and death.

In the church the stakes are different but the needs are similar. In this article, we'll look at how a simple priority with shared authority can be a trellis for the vine and a blessing to the body of Christ.

Unlike a tree or flower, vines need something to grow on. Without support the branches will cling to and follow the direction of anything they can find. Churches are similar: clear structure supports ministry like a trellis, which makes it more likely to be fruitful.

Assuming that's true, a natural question arises: Does the Bible have much to say about church structure? In short, yes! At the core is a biblical understanding of elders, deacons, and church members, and their varied authority and various responsibilities. But is there anything else to say? How can elders, deacons, and church members work together toward a trellis-supported, vine-growing ministry? To answer these questions, let's consider four characteristics of such a ministry.

1. SIMPLICITY

Churches need a structure that everyone can understand. Otherwise, people won't know how to get answers and information. This can produce speculation at best and suspicion at worst. The trellis metaphor is helpful because it's simple. The vine will naturally and easily find its way upward if the trellis is sturdy and straight. People and ministries work similarly. They attach and grow when competent and qualified leaders maintain a simple trellis.

Simplicity also helps a church avoid friction. Complexity leads to confusion, which is a recipe for conflict. The elements of the service, and the work of the ministry should be simple and clearly defined. It's acceptable for churches to be ordinary. The leadership team doesn't need to make elaborate, ever-changing plans. Instead, churches must adhere to what Scripture makes clear, trusting that God will be faithful. This shapes not only the elements of our gatherings but also the shape of our various ministries.

At a personal level, the body grows to appreciate its many members. No one should feel inadequate because of their gifts. Instead, members should exercise the gift(s) they have been given to build up the body. A church member who tries to do everything probably won't do much of anything well. Every member is gifted and should contribute that gift to everyone else. It's that simple.

2. PRIORITY

If the church isn't clear on its mission, it will get distracted. Churches can quickly get off track when they don't know why they exist. So, consider the Lord's requirements for the church. Once we know what he has called us to be, we can deploy human and financial resources to support that mission.

Knowing the mission and means of the church will help churches be less distracted by activities and programs outside their purview. The world is full of parachurch and non-Christian organizations committed to good humanitarian work. But is the church supposed to major in humanitarian work? No, the church's primary mission is to make disciples, and the Bible is our manual for how to do that.

A trellis should set the outer limits for the vine. Trellises informed by mission result in clear objectives. Clear objectives help a church turn down good opportunities to focus on great ones. Everything outside the grow zone is pruned, which allows fruitful branches to grow in the right direction. Do you see how good trellises help focused vines grow? In time, the whole body gains an intuitive sense of why they exist and what they should do.

3. AUTHORITY

Church leaders will maximize the value of the trellis when they responsibly give their authority to others. Constant appeals for permission or funding can become distracting for leaders and burdensome for servants. Instead, leaders should empower others to carry out acts of service for the good of the whole.

Ideally, decision-making is diffused over a larger area. This is beneficial for several reasons. It gives the members a greater sense of ownership as they see the fruit of their meaningful contributions. Members will also be more inclined to use their best judgment for problem-solving, leading to faster fixes. As a result of this, leaders become freed to stay focused on the big picture as watchmen and shepherds.

4. OBJECTIVITY

Church administration involves evaluating ideas, and some will be better than others. As they say, "not all ministry opportunities are created equal!" Without a system made to weigh the merits of an idea, you run the risk of getting sold. An objective leader, working within a sturdy system, will have the tools to call out a bad idea, even if it's his own.

In other words, biblical trellises bring objectivity, which produces stability.

The alternative to a biblical trellis is either structures or trellises manufactured by the leaders themselves to fit their own style or preference; or a lack of structures or trellis, which means the whims and conflicts and personalities of the moment will tend to rule. After all, if ego infects the leadership structure, then the leaders' identity gets intermingled with the church itself. When things go wrong, it can lead to discouragement. When things go well, it can induce pride. In every case it will hinder the church, the leadership, and the flock.

Building biblically, on the other hand, forces every decision through the channels that God intends, not the channels that we make for ourselves and that satisfy our biases.

CONCLUSION

Don't let the vine determine the shape of the trellis. Build out biblically, then grow into it. Structure at the beginning will train the vine. The longest-lasting designs are simple and well-engineered. They started with an end in mind, and everything grows up into a unified whole.

Effective administration requires simple structure, shared priorities, clear lines of authority, and a clear overarching mission. The *result* of effective administration is a healthy and fruitful vine, one that can withstand seasons of difficulty.

ABOUT THE AUTHOR

Jonathan Rourke is the senior pastor of Tri-City Bible Church in Vista, California.

How to Have a Well-Run Elders' Meeting

Aaron Menikoff

COVID-19 changed the way businesses operate. Instead of fighting traffic, sitting in a cubicle, and discussing politics around the water cooler, a growing number of employees push away their Cheerios bowl, pull out their laptop, and work from home. This change comes with risks like lower morale and increased loneliness. However, few object to fewer meetings; boardrooms are seen as spaces where productivity goes to die.

Even as leadership teams in the business world meet less and less, I see the value of church elders regularly being in the same room as they think and pray about their church. In fact, besides the gatherings of our whole church, the most important meeting I attend is our bi-weekly elders' meeting. Every other Thursday night, we convene to pray for church members, discuss urgent shepherding matters, and oversee the affairs of the congregation.

What can we do to make these meetings excellent? The Bible offers no specific guidance on how to have a well-run elders' meeting. However, here are ten encouragements—some principled, some pragmatic—that may be helpful as you start or tweak the elders' meetings at your church.

Do remember: every church is different. An elders' meeting with three elders will probably be a lot less formal than one with thirty! The church I serve is about in the middle. Whatever the size of your church or elder body, I pray these encouragements help you to organize meetings brothers love to attend.

1. Start with godly elders.

This is the most important ingredient in a well-run elders' meeting. Brothers who love the Lord, put the interests of others first, care for the flock, and long to be an encouragement—such men are a delight to bring together and make meetings a joy.

2. Select an organized leader.

Give someone the responsibility to set the agenda, send it out in advance, convene the meeting, and steward the conversation. By "steward the conversation," I mean soliciting input from elders where necessary, limiting discussion when it begins to drag, and even bringing the deliberations to an end by tabling discussion or calling for a vote. An organized leader is a unique blessing to an elder body.

3. Encourage thoughtful, robust, respectful conversation.

An elder who talks too much is a tax on the others. A brother who talks too little underestimates the importance of his contribution. Worst of all is an elder ill-prepared to engage the topic at hand. Good meetings are not just about accomplishing tasks but sharing wisdom—hearing from brothers raised up by the Spirit to shepherd the flock.

4. Make space for organized and organic prayer.

The well-being of the church rests in the hands of our sovereign God. We should implore him to bless the members and ministries of the church. Plan ahead to pray for select members and items (organized prayer). Be willing to interrupt an elders' meeting to plead with God to intervene in a difficult situation (organic prayer). It's unlikely you will ever pray too much. However, short petitions are not ungodly, and a wise elder knows how to keep his prayer brief (see Eccl. 5:1-3; Matt. 6:5).

5. Open the Bible often.

Answers to problems can't always be proof-texted. But sometimes they can! And even when they can't, there are certainly biblical implications we can consider. Therefore, elders should regularly ask, "Does the Bible have anything to say about what we're discussing?" God is the Lord of his church, not the elders. We look to his Word for guidance.

6. Stay focused on spiritual matters.

Labor to prioritize issues that require the input of the men entrusted with the ministry of the Word. If the question-at-hand can be resolved by a deacon, it probably shouldn't be discussed at the elders' meeting. Hit a pinata, and you expect Tootsie Rolls and Smarties to cascade onto the ground. Hit an elders' meeting, and discussions of discipleship, soul care, theology, and future leaders should burst forth.

7. Create a healthy dynamic between staff-elders and lay-elders.

Lay elders should respect the staff elders who have devoted themselves full-time to shepherding the local church. They surely take a significant weight off the shoulders of the elder body by organizing church ministries. It is wise for lay elders to give plenty of room for staff elders to make certain decisions without needing to run them by the entire board. Likewise, staff elders should respect the lay elders, who have equal authority and voices that need to be heard. Staff elders should lean into the wisdom of the lay elders when the elder body is gathered. Generally speaking, staff elders should be slower to speak, recognizing their voices often carry considerable weight.

8. Allow meetings to be brief.

A well-run elders' meeting need not be extraordinarily long. Ours last from 7–9:30 p.m., and our chair works hard to end the meeting on time. This is never easy, and it is only a rule-of-thumb—sometimes pressing matters require we extend the time. However, if all the elders know when we plan to finish, they tend to speak only when necessary and be succinct when they do.

9. Keep substantial conversations to a minimum.

We handle "shepherding matters" and "business" at each elders' meeting. Shepherding matters and prayer typically take more than an hour, leaving about an hour for other business—new elder nominations, mission opportunities, the church budget, etc. To accommodate this schedule, we try to limit business to two or three topics at most. If we need an extended period of time for a particular conversation, we'll either spread it out among several gatherings, save it for an elders' retreat, or hold off until we can have an elders' meeting with that topic as the only agenda item.

10. Utilize elder sub-teams.

Even if our elders' meetings went to 2 a.m., we still wouldn't have the hours we need to get into the weeds as much as we should. Therefore, our chair regularly puts together small groups of elders to deliberate in separate meetings throughout the month before bringing a recommendation to the body as a whole. These groups may discuss prospective missionaries, the upcoming budget, revisions to our statement of faith, and diaconal ministry. They do not replace the elder body as a whole, but their labors grease the wheels for our deliberations and help our meetings run smoothly.

CONCLUSION

There is no silver-bullet to a well-run elders' meeting. Still, this whole list has served our church well as we've operated with elders for over a dozen years. And I can't emphasize enough the importance of godly elders and an organized leader. We are a work in progress, but our meetings are a joy because the work is good and the Christ we serve is glorious.

ABOUT THE AUTHOR

Aaron Menikoff is the senior pastor of Mt. Vernon Baptist Church in Sandy Springs, Georgia.

How To Use a Care List in Elders' and Members' Meetings

Alex Bloomfield

Local churches should prioritize vine work (people) over trellis work (programs). Trellises exist to support the vine. People, not programs, are the mission. But if we're honest, it often feels like trellis issues dominate our time, especially in elders' and members' meetings.

How do we work against that?

There are many ways, and one of them is to use something called a "care list."

WHAT IS A CARE LIST?

A care list is an administrative tool that serves elders and church members in caring for weak, hurting, and straying sheep. It is comprised of members who are experiencing an acute need or are found in unrepentant sin. There's a private version of the list seen only by the elders, and there's a public version of the list that would be known to the whole congregation.

When the public version is used as a church discipline tool, it offers a formal way to obey Jesus's command to "tell it to the church"

(Matthew 18:17), while then providing a space of time to elapse before the final step of "treat[ing] them as a Gentile and a tax collector" (Matthew 18:17). At every step, the goal is for the straying sheep to feel the weight of their sin and its effect on their church. The goal is their repentance and restoration.

USING A CARE LIST IN ELDERS' MEETINGS

A care list begins privately among the elders as a way of identifying the most vulnerable members. It prevents any difficult situations from falling through the cracks. The chairman might say to the room, "Is there anyone you think needs special attention?" This provides every elder the opportunity to raise the matter of a troubled marriage, or of someone who is sowing division, or of an elderly member's failing health.

To put someone on this internal, private list is his way of saying to his fellow elders, "We need to keep our eyes on this, brothers, and make sure we're checking in." It's like a siren or flashing light. It reminds them to pray for and maintain regular contact with these vulnerable sheep.

Once a situation gets added to this list by elder consensus, it stays there for future meetings until the circumstances are resolved.

USING A CARE LIST IN MEMBERS' MEETINGS

Sometimes, when a problem is acute enough, an individual's name will move from the private care list to the public one made known to the members in a members' meeting. And here the list works similarly. It points the church toward significant pressure points and helps them know how best to minister to their fellow members.

Put simply, it's a mobilization tool. It says to the congregation, "Look and minister here!"

During the meeting, the care list would be shared with the congregation. I recommend doing this verbally and not in written format, which is best for confidentiality. An elder should then share a brief rationale or update for each person on the care list, take questions in most cases, and pause to pray for each person.

If someone has been added to the list as part of a discipline process, the congregation should be instructed on how to engage with the member in hopes of restoring them to repentance. For example, the elders may think it wise for only those members with a prior relationship to reach out, while others are exhorted only to pray. In other cases, the elders may think it best for many members to make contact. Either way, the elders should prepare the congregation for the possibility of excommunicating the person at the following meeting should they refuse to repent.

Sometimes, a personal crisis is so severe that a member is added to the care list (cancer diagnosis, house fire, death in the family, etc.). This alerts the congregation to give special support and prayer to their hurting brother or sister. As many battle-tested saints can attest, the worst days of suffering often come after the initial wave of support. When a loved one passes, or someone gets sick, people rush to the scene and rise to the occasion. But what about the weeks following the funeral or the months after the dire diagnosis? A members' meeting care list keeps the congregation's mind and heart on their hurting members.

TWO BENEFITS OF USING A CARE LIST

First, a care list lessens the shock value of an escalating church discipline case and thereby protects leaders from unwarranted accusations. Members can take the necessary time to process the news, share relevant information with elders, and raise questions before exercising the keys of discipline. Church discipline is a sorrowful exercise. While a care list doesn't remove the pain of ex-communication, it does provide a trellis for the necessary work. Rather than feeling forced by elders to act immediately, a care list gives the church time to become informed and to act with freedom and purpose. We know Satan loves to use church discipline to sew division and break down a congregation's trust in its leaders. A care list chokes this tactic by its inherent transparency and intentionality.

Second, a care list engages the whole church in both corrective discipline and caring for the weak. In large congregations, the hurting and the straying can sometimes be hard to see. After all, they're one in hundreds or more! But thankfully, a care list points to serious opportunities to show love and give service.

IS THIS USEFUL FOR A SMALL CHURCH?

If you're like me and come from or pastor a small church, you may think care lists are only necessary for big churches. Does a 50-person church really need a trellis like this? I would suggest that it does. Even small churches can fail to recognize their greatest needs. Because discipline can affect a small church's unity even more than a large church, it may be even more pressing that the leaders of small churches prepare their people well before asking them to make a decision about discipline.

Since discipline is often infrequent in smaller churches, some members may be navigating it for the first time. The shock value may be high, so care lists provide a cushion in the form of time. In most cases, and certainly in small churches, slowing down and being deliberate is the wisest path.

CONCLUSION

We will not regret any extra time spent caring for God's sheep. Yes, a care list may add more time to elders' and members' meetings, but the cost is worth it.

In fact, we should be willing to cut other things to make room for caring for the most vulnerable. Our people are going to dwell forever in heaven or hell. This truth has a focusing force to it. A care list may serve your church to keep the vulnerable safe and rebuke the straying. It's a trellis that supports the vine.

ABOUT THE AUTHOR

Alex Bloomfield is an elder of New City Baptist Church in Toronto.

LGBTQ+ Policies

WHAT DO WE DO ABOUT YOUTH GROUP?

Zach Carter

Last year a few parents asked me for a meeting. They explained that a boy in their kids' school returned from Thanksgiving break identifying as a girl. The school district's policy guaranteed toilet access according to his perceived gender identity. Any female student who felt uncomfortable sharing a stall next to him was required to go to the bathroom in the nurse's office. These kids were in fourth grade.

Every church in the United States has schools in its vicinity that have, are, or most likely will soon experience what the parents at our church experienced. Pastors must disciple their people to think biblically about LGBTQ+ issues. This is especially the case in family ministries. Though discipling involves more than policy, we cannot afford to think it means less. Wise policies allow a congregation to continue gospel ministry in an increasingly pagan culture. Good policies are urgently needed in children and student ministries. The goal of this article is to help us think through what these policies may look like.

SETTING THE STAGE

Policies aren't created in a vacuum, and wise ones consider the moment and questions at hand. Let me set the stage—so to speak—by giving context for my suggestions on the how's and why's of family ministry policy.

In the United States of America, two federal government departments oversee public, independent, and collegiate education: the Department of Education and the Department of Justice. The Department of Education supports local and state school boards' efforts by providing standards and research and by executing laws on education. The Department of Justice ensures that students' constitutional rights are not violated. Furthermore, Congress passed the Education Amendments of 1972 to tie the federal government's prerogatives in education to its funding.

Most Americans are familiar with Title IX of the Education Amendments of 1972. These are statutes inserted into previous legislation to expand protections to students based on sex. The objective was to protect the interests of female students. The law states: "No person in the United States shall, on the basis of sex, be excluded from participation in, be denied the benefits of, or be subjected to discrimination under any educational program or activity receiving Federal financial assistance."[1] There are a few exceptions in application carved out by the statute itself, but in general, the Supreme Court has broadly applied Title IX to protect students' constitutional rights.

Each presidential administration determines how it will execute this law. On March 13, 2016, President Obama's Department of Education and the Department of Justice issued a joint statement indicating that the two departments would consider the interests of LGBTQ+ students to be protected under the Title IX statute. They also offered guidelines on accommodations schools should make to comply, including sports inclusion and protected bathroom/locker room access.[2] The Trump administration revoked this guidance. The Biden administration then reversed course and reapplied the Obama administration's interpretation of the "U.S. Supreme

1 "20 U.S. Code § 1681 – Sex". LII / *Legal Information Institute*. Cornell Law School. Retrieved June 29, 2022. https://www.law.cornell.edu/uscode/text/20/1681.

2 U.S. Department of Justice and U.S. Department of Education, "Dear Colleague Letter on Transgender Students," May 13, 2016, https://www2.ed.gov/about/offices/list/ocr/letters/colleague-201605-title-ix-transgender.pdf

Court decision in *Bostock v. Clayton County*."[3] *Bostock* guaranteed the civil rights of LGBTQ+ employees under the Civil Rights Act. One does not have to stretch the imagination to see why the Biden administration sees a corollary between *Bostock*'s implication and Title IX application. On June 23, 2022, the Department of Education announced future regulations reinforcing Title IX's covering of transgender students.[4]

This is the world in which the next generation is being catechized. This is the world in which family ministries will need to minister.

When I was a student pastor in Louisville, Kentucky, in 2014—before the Obama administration issued its Title IX guidelines—one high school in our area, Atherton High School, took it upon itself to issue LGBTQ+ policies. Atherton parents and administrators moved to grant access to bathrooms and locker rooms to transgender students according to their gender identity. These moves quickly gained influence around the country.

Things moved quickly after that. Students started asking many questions about transgenderism. By 2015, I started advocating for our church leadership to act. During this time, we were partnered with a parachurch organization to gain gospel opportunities on our local high school's campus. Following one summer break, a room in the library had been converted into an LGBTQ+ safe space with signage and a 3' x 5' pride flag. Our ministry teams began seeing an increase in students experimenting with same-sex relationships. Back at church, our students were persistently talking about issues related to sexuality. They wanted to know what the Bible taught.

I approached my senior pastor with a proposed statement for our ministry handbook on human sexuality and gender. We needed policies for things like locker rooms, bathrooms, camp sleeping arrangements, dress codes, and

3 U.S. Department of Education, "U.S. Department of Education Confirms Title IX Protects Students from Discrimination Based on Sexual Orientation and Gender Identity," Press Release, June 15, 2021, https://www.ed.gov/news/press-releases/us-department-education-confirms-title-ix-protects-students-discrimination-based-sexual-orientation-and-gender-identity.

4 Moriah Balingit and Nick Anderson, "Sweeping Title IX changes would shield trans students, abuse survivors," *Washington Post*, June 23, 2022, https://www.washingtonpost.com/education/2022/06/23/title-ix-biden-trans-sexual-assault-college/.

more. After all, we want unsaved kids to come to our church events, so we wrote policies that applied to believers and nonbelievers as a condition for participation. Most importantly, I did not want Title IX regulations to catechize my volunteers, families, or children on how the church should handle real-world scenarios. We thought having a stated and adopted policy would give us more significant standing should someone accuse us of discrimination.

So, on December 22, 2016, we added the following policy to our student ministry handbook. We weren't trying to reinvent the wheel and lifted some of the sentences directly out of a policy drafted by Southern Seminary. As I am no longer on staff at that church, I have anonymized it for their privacy:

> [Our student ministry's] policy regarding sexuality and gender identity is grounded in the orthodox understanding of Christian sexuality, which is rooted in the Bible. We confess that sex and gender are gifts from God. At birth, a human being is born as either a physiological male or a physiological female; by extension, gender is an immutable, exclusively binary characteristic rooted in the physiology of each human being. Any blurring of the boundary between maleness and femaleness, such as identifying oneself as a transvestite, transsexual, or transgendered, is contrary to biblical standards. We also confess any sexual orientation other than strict heterosexuality to be a deviation from God's good design for human sexuality.
>
> In the event that a student presents a gender different than his or her biological sex, we expect them – when involved in [our] official and unofficial events – to live and present in accord with their biologically assigned sex. This includes but is not limited to pronouns, dress, appropriate bathrooms, locker rooms, assigned sleeping arrangements, groupings, classes, etc. We must view the actions or intentions of those seeking fundamental changes of any kind from one's sex at birth as a rejection of the biblical and theological understandings to which

[our congregation] is committed and hence as grounds for removal from activities and the Student Ministry. The same is true for persistent or exaggerated examples of cross-dressing and other expressions or actions that are deliberately discordant with birth sex. Decisions will be handled on a case-by-case basis in a pastorally sensitive manner. Every case should be brought to the attention of the Student Pastor immediately before any correction takes place.

No student, however, will be turned away from any event because he or she struggles with his or her gender identity or sexual orientation. We welcome everyone [to our gatherings] as long as he or she is working toward a repentant, life-transforming relationship with Jesus Christ that is obedient to the ethical demands of the Old and New Testaments.

Volunteers are expected to be compassionate, understanding that the culture has confused (and lied!) to so many image-bearers about the nature of gender and sexuality. They are to compassionately explain our policies and lovingly invite them to participate even if the student feels uncomfortable presenting something other than their own perceived gender. Only after manifold, compassionate exhortations to repent and experience the life-transforming grace of the Lord Jesus Christ will students be asked to no longer participate in [our] student activities.

See, "XVIII. The Family," Baptist Faith and Message 2000.

See "Transgender Identity" (http://www.sbc.net/resolutions/2250/on-transgender-identity).[5]

We needed to clearly address our city's cultural moment and teach our volunteers to have compassion for confused children. This policy helped us strike a balance between these two things.

POLICIES SERVE PASTORS

Every day, over 2,000 airplanes fly across the Atlantic Ocean with little help from ground radar or air traffic control. Why are there no

5 This link is no longer active, but this reference was included in the original policy.

collisions? Because of a policy—a treaty called North Atlantic Tracks (NAT-OTS). Spaced ten minutes apart, planes enter and follow the tracks at assigned waypoints created the day before. The NAT-OS dramatically reduces the risk of collision due to spotty radar coverage. More importantly, it also reduces the decision fatigue of airline pilots.

Policies function similarly in the life of a congregation; they wisely delegate decision-making. Generally, most pastors don't enter ministry eager to write policies. Furthermore, few congregations consider administrative prowess as an important pastoral characteristic. And yet, God gifted administrators to his church.

Paul listed "administrating" as one of the gifts for the church (1 Cor. 12:28). Contrary to common perception, its scope is more significant than spreadsheets and expense reports. The word overlaps with concepts like navigation, and LXX translators used the same word to translate Proverbs 1:5; 11:14; and 24:6. Each of these verses celebrates the virtue of someone who can guide a group through difficult circumstances.

Clear policies reduce the potential for collision and decision fatigue. This isn't to say that policies pastor people on their own. However, policies create decision lanes, reducing collisions. A policy might indeed discriminate, but a good policy discriminates without respect for persons. For example, a policy may say, "you have a bad driving record, so you can't drive our church bus." Additionally, a policy reduces decision fatigue by automating a course of action. Like waypoints across the Atlantic, policies provide guidance where details might be lacking.

Increasingly, pastors will be asked to make complex moral decisions related to LGBTQ+ issues. Policies delegate the decision-making process, creating more time for pastors to exhort, instruct, and disciple individuals on gender identity and sexual orientation.

POLICIES MAKE NARROW ROADS STRAIGHT

Policies are not precisely like autopilots. They are more like teachers.

Pastoring people who have been discipled by the constant voice of corporate or educational policies is challenging. Yesterday, I went to lunch with a major in the armed forces. He shared that he had recently been required to take a training session on new policies for transgender soldiers' physical training. Apparently, they would be evaluated according to whether they were "pre-op" or "post-op." Let the one who has ears hear.

A good policy does two things. First, it identifies a biblical principle with requisite support. Second, it bends that principle into an application. In other words, a policy connects how the Bible should be obeyed in a specific real-world scenario.

Increasingly, church members will be shaped by policies from their vocational domains. This means they will have a different autopilot; different waypoints will influence their instincts. Good policies in the church allow pastors to multiply their teaching impact by neutralizing disordered policies in the world.

WHAT COMES NEXT?

I introduced my 2016 ministry handbook with these words:

"The gospel has always been the hub through which ordinary people turn the world upside down. We have the most precious opportunity to call our people to a radical, counter-cultural revolution that emphasizes others over "friends," speaking the truth in love over "likes," and following Christ over their own "followers."

I'm convinced there hasn't been a more exciting, urgent, rewarding, challenging, and frustrating time to be in ministry. I'm glad you are joining us."

Policies aren't as glamorous as preaching. But as far as they protect and teach our people, they are important.

ABOUT THE AUTHOR

Zach Carter is a discipleship pastor of Rivertree Church in Huntsville, Alabama.

Sabbaticals for the Shepherds

Garrett Kell

> *"Rest time is not waste time. It is economy to gather fresh strength. . . . It is wisdom to take occasional furlough."*
>
> – Charles Spurgeon, "The Minister's Fainting Fits"

All work is hard, but faithful pastoral ministry takes a unique toll on the laborer. Pastors have the exhausting honor of carrying the daily pressure of anxiety for the church (2 Cor. 11:28). Office hours are not sufficient for the unceasing strain of broken marriages, straying sinners, suffering saints, and spiritual warfare.

This is why it's wise for churches to require rest for their pastors. I'm not talking about a day off (which pastors should guard) or a vacation (which pastors should take) but a required season of rest known as a sabbatical.

PURPOSE

Churches are served best by invigorated shepherds. When a pastor is rested and refreshed in Christ, his oversight will be infused with wisdom, forbearance, and compassion. But exhausted and burned-out shepherds have little to give. Their patience runs short, and cynicism runs high. This manner of ministry isn't good for anyone (Heb. 13:7).

Wisely scheduled sabbaticals can prevent burnout by providing an opportunity to step away from regular routines. These sabbaticals are not glorified vacations. They may include vacation-like elements, but their aim is uniquely rest and rejuvenation for the soul. Sabbaticals allow pastors to cease normal duties, lay down taxing burdens, and reshape existing rhythms to press deeper into God's grace. In this way, sabbaticals serve both sheep and shepherd.

POLICY

A sabbatical policy sets expectations for everyone. As a minister who loves my calling, I am helped by parameters that require me to rest. I've joked that my elders "sabbatical me" from time-to-time because they know when I need to retreat and be refreshed in the Lord.

Some churches pattern pastoral sabbaticals after the seventh-day rest of the Old Testament. This means every seven years, a pastor takes sabbatical leave. This may serve some pastors well, but I have found more frequent sabbatical plans to be wiser.

The policy should aim to avoid burnout instead of responding to it. For instance, our staff pastors accrue three weeks of sabbatical leave for every year of employment completed. This allows us to take nine weeks off every three years or 12 weeks off every four years.

Implementing a policy like this requires teaching the congregation. Some churches will immediately understand the wisdom of a sabbatical, but others may be suspicious. Teaching through the pastoral epistles and related passages helps the flock understand the colossal responsibility pastors carry (Heb. 13:17, 1 Pet. 5:1–11).

It may also be helpful for the pastor and his wife (if he's married) to share with the congregation how they experience ministry. Without grumbling, they can explain that pastors are often required to be "on the clock" far past office hours, bear the weight of others' sin and suffering, and face criticism from those same sheep. As Jared C. Wilson said, "Good pastors can't take the pastor hat off at the end of the day or leave their hearts for their flocks in the office when they clock out. It's not something you can just turn off."

PLAN

To best steward a sabbatical, pastors should develop a plan. He should work with his family and elders to come up with goals and a travel schedule. Goals may include a devotional plan, family time, physical rest, exercise, diet, counseling, studying, and writing. The plan should not be overly ambitious so the pastor actually rests.

The congregation should also consider how to bless their pastors during the time away. This may involve writing letters of encouragement, setting up a prayer calendar to intercede for him, providing a stipend to alleviate expenses, or offering air miles or vacation homes to facilitate travel.

Before leaving, the pastor should ensure all his counseling cases and teaching responsibilities are entrusted to others. This is the time to lean on fellow pastors, aspiring pastors, or pastors in your broader network for help. And he should consider making plans for reentry, such as meeting with staff and elders for updates on anything he needs to be caught up on.

PRINCIPLES

Developing a sabbatical requires wisdom. As you make your plans, consider the counsel other pastors have shared with me.

1. Don't rely on sabbaticals to stay zealous. Shepherds are first sheep. If we forget this, spiritual exhaustion is unavoidable. Always aim to minister from the overflow of your fellowship with Jesus (John 15:1–11).
2. Rest but don't rust. You can unplug from regular rhythms of ministry in a way that doesn't end up edifying. Properly enjoying movies, games, sports, and entertainment is possible, but so is abusing them. Remember: you will end up loving what you retreat to for rest. Keep entertainment in its proper place, and always aim to enjoy Jesus, who promises lasting rest for your weary soul (Matt. 11:28).

3. If possibly achievable, leave town for at least part of the sabbatical. You may not get to the south of France like Spurgeon, but somewhere ministry won't be constantly pulling at you is helpful. At the same time, don't travel too much, as that itself can be taxing.
4. Perhaps visit other gospel-preaching churches instead of your own. For some pastors, unplugging can be difficult at your own church. Attending other like-minded local churches can refresh, encourage, and inspire creative ideas for your own church.
5. Sabbaticals are as much for the pastor's wife as for the pastor. She needs a break, too. Member, find creative ways to bless the pastor's whole family. Pastor, consider personal and marriage counseling. Even if things are going well, having a professional help you process personal and pastoral pressures can be life-giving.
6. Withdraw from *everything* to focus on *some things*. Guard extended time in prayer and the Scriptures. Your great aim is to draw nearer to Jesus.

   Make modest goals to write, study, or plan to that end. But be careful not to begin projects that will stress you later. Returning from sabbatical with half-finished projects sets you up for future trouble.
7. Read life-giving material. Aside from Scripture, develop a list of other books and articles you hope to consume. Don't measure success by how much you read, but by how deeply you commune with the Lord through what you read.
8. Don't "talk shop" with fellow elders during your time off. I was notorious for trying to ask leading questions to my elders to get any information about what was happening, but they were joyfully tight-lipped to shield me from any news. It was a kindness I remain thankful for.

CONCLUSION

Sabbaticals are no substitute for regular patterns of rest and refreshment in Christ, but they can serve a pastor's soul toward a long, faithful ministry.

If you haven't thought much about the need for a pastor to rest, you may want to read Charles Spurgeon's article "The Minister's Fainting Fits" and Christopher Ash's book *Zeal without Burnout*.

ABOUT THE AUTHOR

Garrett Kell is the lead pastor of Del Ray Baptist Church in Alexandria, Virginia. You can find him on Twitter at @pastorjgkell.

Sample Constitution and Elder Meeting Bylaws

3ABC CONSTITUTION

Since it pleased Almighty God, by His Holy Spirit, to call certain of His servants to unite here in 1894 under the name [NAME OF CHURCH] of [CITY, STATE] for the worship of God and the spread of the gospel of Jesus Christ, and since He has sustained and prospered this work to the present day; and

Whereas we, having searched the Scriptures under the guidance of His Spirit, have recognized the need to reconstitute ourselves to conform more closely to His will for the Church in this age and to prepare ourselves for greater efforts in His name;

Now therefore, we do hereby organize ourselves in accord with the [any relevant State requirements] and adopt this Constitution as our articles of governance, to be interpreted at all times to reflect the character of and bring glory to Jesus Christ, as revealed in the Holy Bible and articulated in the Statement of Faith and Covenant of this church.

ARTICLE 1. MEMBERSHIP

Section 1.

Clause 1. Members of this church shall be believers in Jesus Christ Who give evidence of regeneration;

Clause 2. Who have been baptized as believers in obedience to Christ;

Clause 3. Who hold without mental reservation the doctrines of our church as expressed in the Statement of Faith; and

Clause 4. Who promise to keep the commitments expressed in the Church Covenant.

Section 2.

Clause 1. An Applicant shall be received as a Member of the church upon the recommendation of the Elders and the subsequent agreement of at least three-quarters of the Members present and voting on the question at any Members' Meeting.

Clause 2. No Member of this church shall retain membership in any other church.

Section 3.

Clause 1. Members shall be expected to participate actively in the life of the church By regularly attending its Lord's Day meetings;

Clause 2. By faithfully observing its ordinances, namely Baptism and the Lord's Supper;

Clause 3. By submitting to its discipline and instruction; and

Clause 4. By attending, as frequently as possible, its Members' Meetings.

Clause 5. No Person who is not a Member or Church Associate shall lead any ministry or hold any office of the church.

As amended by the congregation, 4/15/2020 (Multiple). Amended 4/22/2015 (§3.2.6, §3.5.5). Amended 9/18/2013 (§1.3.6, §3.2.1). Amended 5/16/2012 (§3.2.6, §3.2.15, §3.4, §4.1.2, §4.2). Amended 4/20/2011 (§3.2.2, §3.3.2, §3.4.2). Amended 10/17/07 (§1.4.3). Amended 12/20/06 (§4.2.5). Amended 7/19/06 (§3.2.8). Implemented 3/15/06. Adopted 2/15/06.

Section 4.

Clause 1. The church shall recognize the termination of a Person's

Membership following his or her death, and may do so following his or her voluntary resignation or joining with another church.

Clause 2. The church shall have authority to exercise discipline over its Members, which may involve excluding from its Membership any Member consistently neglectful of the duties enumerated in Article 1, Sections 1 and 3, or guilty of scandalous conduct by which the reputation of Christ or His church is dishonored. Any such action shall be done in accordance with the instructions of the Lord Jesus in Matthew 18:15-17 and those of the Apostle Paul in 1 Corinthians 5:1-5 and 2 Corinthians 2:6-8.

Clause 3. The church shall have authority to refuse a Member's voluntary resignation or transfer of membership to another church, either for the purpose of proceeding with a process of church discipline, or for any other reason the church deems necessary or prudent.

Clause 4. A Member shall be removed from Membership as a matter of church discipline upon the recommendation of the Elders and the subsequent agreement of at least three-quarters of the Members present and voting on the question at any Members' Meeting.

Section 5.

Clause 1. Students and others temporarily residing in the Louisville area may be received as Associates of the church, provided they are members in good standing of another evangelical Baptist church.

Clause 2. An Applicant shall be received as an Associate upon the recommendation of the Elders and the subsequent agreement of at least three-quarters of the Members present and voting on the question at any Members' Meeting.

Clause 3. Associates shall retain membership in one other evangelical and baptistic church.

Clause 4. Associates shall be expected to participate actively in the life of the church in the same way as Members, except that they shall not be eligible either to stand for any office or to vote.

Clause 5. A Person's Association with the church shall

terminate immediately upon the ending of residence in the Louisville area or by voluntary resignation. The church shall have authority to terminate the Association of any Church Associate consistently neglectful of his or her duties, or guilty of scandalous conduct by which the reputation of Christ or His church is dishonored. In such an event, the Elders shall refer disciplinary action to the pastor or elders of the excluded person's home church.

ARTICLE 2. MEETINGS

Section 1.

The church shall meet together for public worship each Lord's Day morning, and at other times throughout the week as the church may determine.

Section 2.

Clause 1. The church shall hold a regular Members' Meeting at least every other month, which shall not be held in place of the regular Lord's Day morning meeting, but at some other time.

Clause 2. The Elders, whenever they deem it necessary, or within thirty days of receiving a written request signed by ten percent of the voting Membership, shall call a special Members' Meeting.

Clause 3. No Members' Meeting shall be held until the date, time, and place of such meeting shall be announced at every public meeting of the church for one week immediately prior to the Members' Meeting in question, except as described in section 4.2.3 of this Constitution.

Clause 4. The Chairman of the Elders or his Representative shall preside as Moderator at all Members' Meetings, but shall have no vote, unless the Members be equally divided on a question.

Clause 5. Members' Meetings shall proceed according to a reasonable order, and the Members present shall constitute a quorum to do business. Motions shall be adopted upon the agreement of a majority of the Members present and voting on the question, except on matters otherwise provided for in this constitution.

Clause 6. Members must be physically present in order to Vote. For the purposes of this Constitution, "present" shall be defined as physically present.

Clause 7. In the event that legal orders by local, state, or federal officials would prevent the Church from holding at least bi-monthly Members' Meetings as required by this Constitution, and the Elders agree to abide by those orders, the Moderator shall declare duly-called meetings to be "virtual." In that case, all requirements in this Constitution for physical presence at Members' Meetings shall be waived, and the Church shall gather and conduct business by any technological means available to the majority of the Church. No other rule shall be affected by a virtual meeting.

Section 3.

Clause 1. The church, duly assembled in a Members' Meeting, shall be responsible To elect officers;

Clause 2. To receive Applicants into church Membership;

Clause 3. To recognize termination of Membership due to death, transfer of Membership, or voluntary resignation;

Clause 4. To exercise church discipline;

Clause 5. To approve, once in every year, a church budget;

Clause 6. To hear reports from the Elders and, from time to time, the various Deacons/Deaconesses; and

Clause 7. To take any other action they deem necessary or desirable.

ARTICLE 3. GOVERNMENT

Section 1.

The biblical offices in the church shall be Elders and Deacons, but final earthly authority is vested in the assembled congregation.

Section 2.

Clause 1. Oversight of the ministry, resources, and facilities of the church shall be vested in a Council of Elders, which shall be comprised of not fewer than three men who satisfy the qualifications set forth in 1 Timothy 3:1-7 and Titus 1:6-9.

Clause 2. Elders shall be selected as follows: The Council of Elders shall at any regular Members' Meeting present to the church a list of nominees to the office of Elder. For a period of at least one month, the church shall consider whether such nominees are qualified for the office. If any Member believes one or more of the nominees to be unqualified, that Member shall express such concern to the Elders, who may on the basis of that advice remove names from the list of nominees. No name shall be added to the list of nominees which was not included on the initial list. When a period of one month has elapsed, the Elders shall at the next regular Members' Meeting present a final list of nominees to the church, who shall vote Yea or Nay on each of the nominees in turn. The Moderator or his delegates shall count the votes, and any nominee having the approval of at least three-quarters of the Members present and voting on his nomination shall be an Elder, which men the church shall in due haste publicly recognize and set apart as such.

Clause 3. At least once in every year, the Elders shall at any regular Members' Meeting solicit from the congregation recommendations for the office of Elder, which recommendations shall be given to the Elders in private, and not publicly. The Elders shall give due consideration to any recommendation received.

Clause 4. In accordance with 1 Timothy 2:12 and 3:2, women shall not serve as Elders.

Clause 5. A majority of the Elders shall be laymen, that is, church members not in the regular pay of the church.

Clause 6. With the exceptions of the Senior Pastor and Associate Pastors, as defined in sections 3.3 and 3.4 of this Constitution, Elders shall be reaffirmed by the church triennially, in accordance with the process described in section 3.2.2 of this Constitution, and having served two consecutive three-year terms, shall not be eligible for re-election for one year. Neither the Senior Pastor nor Associate Pastors shall be subject to a reaffirmation vote, nor to any term limit.

Clause 7. No Elder shall hold the office of Deacon during his tenure.

Clause 8. The Council of Elders shall choose their Chairman and other Officers and shall adopt their own By-Laws. In compliance with the nonprofit corporation laws of Kentucky, the Council of Elders shall serve as the Board of Directors of the Corporation, and the Chairman of the Elders shall serve as the president of the corporation.

Clause 9. Every Elder shall be expected to abide by the By-Laws of the Elder Board of [NAME OF CHURCH], and every Elder shall have a right to attend the entirety of every meeting of the Board, except as described in the By-Laws of the Elder Board of [NAME OF CHURCH].

Clause 10. The Elders shall, in keeping with the principles set forth in the Scriptures, especially Acts 6:1-6; 1 Timothy 3:1-7; 5:17; Titus 1:5-9; James 5:14; and 1 Peter 5:1-4, undertake the responsibility of shepherding God's flock by devoting themselves to prayer and the ministry of the Word. They shall have particular authority To plan and oversee worship services;

Clause 11. To oversee the ordinances, namely Baptism and the Lord's Supper;

Clause 12. To examine and instruct prospective members;

Clause 13. To oversee the process of church discipline;

Clause 14. To examine and recommend candidates for all offices and positions;

Clause 15. To oversee the work of the Deacons/Deaconesses and all other agents of the church;

Clause 16. To hire, oversee, evaluate the performance of, and when necessary terminate paid church staff; and

Clause 17. To take any other action which shall be necessary and proper for faithfully overseeing and shepherding the church.

Clause 18. An Elder shall be removed from office upon the vote of two-thirds of the Members present and voting on the question at any Members' Meeting. Any such action shall be done in accordance with the instructions of the Lord Jesus in Matthew 18:15-17 and those of the Apostle Paul in 1 Timothy 5:17-21.

Clause 19. In the event that the Church has no Elders, the Church shall at the next Regular Members' Meeting elect an Interim Moderator, who shall at each subsequent Regular Members' Meeting nominate one or more men to serve as Elders, pursuant to section 3.2.2 of this Constitution, until an Elder is elected. The office of Interim Moderator shall dissolve immediately upon the election of an Elder.

Section 3.

Clause 1. Primary responsibility for preaching and teaching the Scriptures in public meetings of the church may be vested in a Senior Pastor. Only one Senior Pastor may be recognized at a time.

Clause 2. The Senior Pastor shall be selected as follows: The Elders shall at any regular Members' Meeting present to the church the name of one nominee to the position of Senior Pastor. For a period of at least two weeks, the church shall consider the nominee's gifts in preaching and teaching, and his commitment to minister personally to the members of this church. If any Member believes the nominee to be unqualified, that Member shall express such concern to the Elders. When a period of two weeks has elapsed, the Elders shall at the next Members' Meeting present the nominee for Senior Pastor to the church, who shall vote Yea or Nay on his selection as such. The Moderator or his delegates shall count the votes, and if the nominee receives the approval of at least three-quarters of the Members present and voting on the question, he shall be a Member of the church, an Elder, and the Senior Pastor, whom the church shall in due haste publicly recognize as such.

Clause 3. The Senior Pastor shall meet all the qualifications and hold all the rights and responsibilities of a Member of the church. He shall satisfy all the qualifications and hold all the duties and responsibilities of an Elder. In terms of formal authority, there shall be no distinction between an Elder and the Senior Pastor.

Clause 4. The Senior Pastor shall not be subject to a reaffirmation vote, nor to any term limit.

Clause 5. The Senior Pastor shall be removed from office and his employment terminated upon the vote of two-thirds of the Members present and voting on the question at any Members' Meeting. Any such action shall be done in accordance with the instructions of the Lord Jesus in Matthew 18:15-17 and those of the Apostle Paul in 1 Timothy 5:17-21.

Section 4.

Clause 1. Other particular pastoral responsibilities expected to be of a long-term nature may be vested in one or more Associate Pastors. Other particular pastoral responsibilities expected to be of a short-term nature may be vested in one or more Assistant Pastors.

Clause 2. An Associate Pastor or an Assistant Pastor shall be selected as follows: The Elders shall at any regular Members' Meeting present to the church the name of one nominee to the position of Associate Pastor or Assistant Pastor. For a period of at least two weeks, the church shall consider the nominee's gifts in the particular area of service to which he is being called, and his commitment to minister personally to the members of this church. If any Member believes the nominee to be unqualified, that Member shall express such concern to the Elders. When a period of two weeks has elapsed, the Elders shall at the next Members' Meeting present the nominee for Associate Pastor or Assistant Pastor to the church, who shall vote Yea or Nay on his selection as such. The Moderator or his delegates shall count the votes, and if the nominee receives the approval of at least three-quarters of the Members present and voting on the question, he shall be a Member of the church, an Elder, and an Associate Pastor or Assistant Pastor, whom the church shall in due haste publicly recognize as such.

Clause 3. An Associate Pastor or Assistant Pastor shall meet all the qualifications and hold all the rights and responsibilities of a Member of the church. He shall satisfy all the qualifications and hold all the duties and responsibilities of an Elder. In terms of formal authority, there shall be no distinction between an Elder and an Associate Pastor or Assistant Pastor.

Clause 4. An Associate Pastor shall not be subject to a reaffirmation vote, nor to any term limit. An Assistant Pastor shall be subject to the provisions of section 3.2.6 of this Constitution.

Clause 5. An Associate Pastor or Assistant Pastor shall be

removed from office and his employment terminated upon the vote of two-thirds of the Members present and voting on the question at any Members' Meeting. Any such action shall be done in accordance with the instructions of the Lord Jesus in Matthew 18:15-17 and those of the Apostle Paul in 1 Timothy 5:17-21.

Section 5.

Clause 1. Particular service to the church shall be provided by Deacons/Deaconesses, the number of which shall vary as the church has need, and who shall satisfy the qualifications set forth in 1 Timothy 3:8-13.

Clause 2. The Deacons/Deaconesses shall not meet together regularly as a body. Each diaconate position shall serve a particular need of the church, and shall be created or dissolved upon the recommendation of the Elders and the subsequent agreement of a majority of the Members present and voting on the question at any Members' Meeting.

Clause 3. Deacons/Deaconesses shall be selected as follows: The Council of Elders shall at any regular Members' Meeting present to the church a list of nominees to the office of deacon/deaconess. For a period of at least one month, the church shall consider whether such nominees are qualified for the office. If any Member believes one or more of the nominees to be unqualified, that Member shall express such concern to the Elders, who may on the basis of that advice remove names from the list of nominees. No name shall be added to the list of nominees which was not included on the initial list. When a period of one month has elapsed, the Elders shall at the next regular Members' Meeting present a final list of nominees to the church, who shall vote Yea or Nay on each of the nominees in turn. The Moderator or his delegates shall count the votes, and any nominee having the approval of two-thirds of the Members present and voting on his nomination shall be a Deacon/Deaconess, which men or women the church shall in due haste publicly recognize and set apart as such.

Clause 4. At least once in every year, the Elders shall at any regular Members' Meeting solicit from the congregation recommendations for new diaconate positions and for qualified persons to fill new or vacant positions, which recommendations shall be given to the Elders in private, and not publicly. The Elders shall give due consideration to any recommendation received.

Clause 5. No Deacon shall hold the office of Elder during his or her term, nor more than one Diaconate.

Clause 6. Deacons/Deaconesses shall be reaffirmed by the church triennially, in accordance with the process described in section 3.5.3 of this Constitution.

Clause 7. In keeping with the principles set forth in Acts 6:1-6, Deacons/Deaconesses shall not exercise a ministry of spiritual authority, but shall support the Elders' ministry of the Word, work to maintain the unity of the church, and care for the physical needs of the church.

Clause 8. The church may recognize Deacons/Deaconesses to take responsibility For seeing that the sick, the sorrowing, the aged, and the infirm receive spiritual and physical comfort;

Clause 9. For leading the hospitality ministries of the church;

Clause 10. For attending to the normal care and maintenance of church properties;

Clause 11. For receiving, holding, and disbursing a fund for benevolence, and for reporting from time to time on the use of such funds to both the Elders and the church;

Clause 12. For attending to the accommodations for public worship;

Clause 13. For assisting in distributing the elements during the Lord's Supper; and

Clause 14. For serving in other specific capacities as the church has need.

Clause 15. No person or group shall solicit money on behalf of the church or any of its ministries without the approval of the Elders and the Deacon/Deaconess of Finance.

Clause 16. A Deacon/Deaconess may be removed from office by a decision of the Elders, or upon the recommendation of the Elders and the subsequent agreement of a majority of the Members present and voting on the question at any Members' Meeting, except as otherwise specified by this Constitution.

Clause 17. In the event a diaconate position becomes vacant, the Elders may appoint a person to fill that position and assume its responsibilities, until such time as some person can be duly recognized by the church as a Deacon/Deaconess, but not longer than two consecutive Members' Meetings.

ARTICLE 4. ADMINISTRATION

Section 1.

The church shall select a Deacon/Deaconess of Records, who shall record the minutes of all regular and special Members' Meetings of the church, keep an accurate roll of the membership, and give reports as requested by the Elders, particular Deacons/Deaconesses, or the church. In compliance with the nonprofit corporation laws of Kentucky, the Deacon/Deaconess of Records shall serve as the secretary of the corporation.

Section 2

Clause 1. The church shall select a Deacon/Deaconess of Finance, who shall, with the advice and approval of the Elders, move to the church at the penultimate regular Members' Meeting of every fiscal year a budget, which shall be considered and voted upon by the church at the final regular Members' Meeting of every fiscal year.

Clause 2. The budget shall be adopted upon the motion of the Deacon/Deaconess of Finance and the subsequent agreement of a majority of the Members present and voting on the question.

Clause 3. In the event of a failure by the Church to approve a new Budget by the beginning of the new Fiscal Year, church Staff shall continue to be compensated as specified by the most recent adopted Budget, with its amendments, but no other spending shall be authorized until such time as a new Budget is adopted at any Members' Meeting. In such an event, the Elders may call Special Members' Meetings, their sole order of business being the consideration of a Budget, with one day's notice by Correspondence to the Members of the Church.

Clause 4. Once adopted, the total amount budgeted shall not be overspent. The Elders shall have responsibility to oversee and faithfully disburse the budget. Amendments to the budget shall be adopted upon the motion of the Deacon/Deaconess of Finance and the subsequent agreement of a majority of the Members present and voting on the question at any Members' Meeting.

Clause 5. Oversight of and authority over all other resources of the church shall be vested in the assembled congregation. Upon the recommendation of the elders and the subsequent agreement of a majority of the Members present and voting on the question at any Members' Meeting, the congregation may fund certain designated accounts, distinct from the operating budget, which shall be under the oversight and authority of the Elders.

Section 3.

Clause 1. The church shall select a Deacon/Deaconess of the Treasury, who shall ensure that all funds and securities of the church are properly secured in such banks, financial institutions, or depositories as designated by the church. The Deacon/Deaconess of the Treasury shall also ensure that full and accurate accounts of receipts and disbursements are kept in books belonging to the church, and that adequate controls are implemented to guarantee that all funds belonging to the church are appropriately handled by any officer, employee, or agent of the church. The Deacon/Deaconess of the Treasury shall render to the Elders at least once in every year, or whenever they may require it, an account of all financial transactions and of the financial condition of the church. The Deacon/Deaconess of the Treasury shall also be responsible for presenting regular reports of the account balances, revenues, and expenses of the church at regular Members' Meetings.

Clause 2. No Person shall serve more than one consecutive three-year term as Deacon/Deaconess of the Treasury.

Clause 3. No paid staff member of the church shall be eligible for the office of Deacon/Deaconess of the Treasury.

Clause 4. The Deacon/Deaconess of the Treasury shall be removed from office only upon the recommendation of the Elders and the subsequent agreement of a majority of the Members present and voting on the question at any Members' Meeting.

ARTICLE 5. RATIFICATION

This Constitution shall be ratified upon the approval of two-thirds of the Members present and voting on the question at any regular business meeting of the church, and shall take effect upon the recognition of at least three Elders.

ARTICLE 6. AMENDMENTS

Section 1.

The Statement of Faith or Church Covenant shall be amended upon the recommendation of the Elders and the subsequent agreement of three-quarters of the Members voting on the question at any regular Members' Meeting, provided the Amendment shall have been offered in writing at any previous regular Members' Meeting, and shall have been announced at every public meeting of the church for two weeks immediately prior to final consideration. Any Member serving under the commission of this church on an international mission field shall also be eligible to vote by correspondence on this question.

Section 2.

This Constitution shall be amended by a vote of three-quarters of the Members voting on the question at any regular Members' Meeting, provided the Amendment shall have been offered in writing at any previous regular Members' Meeting, and shall have been announced at every public meeting of the church for two weeks immediately prior to final consideration. Any Member serving under the commission of this church on an international mission field shall also be eligible to vote by correspondence on this question.

◇◇

4.1 ELDER BOARD BY-LAWS

ARTICLE 1. GENERAL

Section 1.

These By-Laws shall be subordinate to the Constitution of [NAME OF CHURCH].

Section 2.

The Elder Board of [NAME OF CHURCH] shall proceed according to a reasonable order. Any question not otherwise governed by these By-Laws shall be determined by a majority vote of the Elders present and voting on the question at any meeting. Except as otherwise specified by any Article of these By-Laws, abstentions shall be considered as absences and therefore deducted from the total number of votes, and Votes shall be considered Final unless a majority of the Body which originally voted on the Question agrees to Reconsider; such a Motion to Reconsider must be made by an Elder who voted with the original Majority or who did not vote on the question.

Section 3.

A Quorum of the Elder Board shall be defined as a Majority of the Full Number of Elders, gathered physically in accordance with Article 3 of these By-Laws, except as otherwise specified by any Article of these By-Laws.

Section 4.

Except as otherwise specified by any Article of these By-Laws, Elders must be physically present in order to Vote. For the purposes of these By-Laws, "present" shall be defined as physically present.

Section 5.

The Full Number of Elders shall be defined as all currently serving Elders, not merely those present. Unanimous Consent shall be defined as the unanimous agreement of the Full Number of Elders, except where otherwise specified in these By-Laws. Votes of the Full Number may be taken, and Unanimous Consent may be obtained, by Correspondence.

Section 6.

Except as otherwise specified by these By-Laws, in lieu of a meeting and on questions of a time-sensitive nature and expected to be non-controversial, the Elders may conduct business by Correspondence. A Vote by Correspondence shall be initiated upon the motion and second of any item of business by any Elder. A Vote by Correspondence shall be considered Final one day after initiation, at which point the question shall be decided by a majority of those voting, or immediately when the question has been decided by a Two-Thirds Majority of the Full Number of Elders. Any Elder may, while a vote by Correspondence is still open and by appeal to the Chairman, refer the question to the next Meeting of the Board.

Section 7.

During the months of March, April, and May of 2020, the Chairman may declare duly-called meetings to be "virtual." In that case, all requirements in these By-Laws for physical presence shall be waived, and the Elders shall be allowed to gather and vote by any technological means available. No other rule shall be affected by a virtual meeting.

ARTICLE 2. OFFICERS

Section 1.

The Senior Pastor, as defined by §3.3 of the Constitution, shall serve as the Chairman and Secretary of the Elder Board. His duties shall be as defined by custom and the provisions of these By-Laws.

Section 2.

The Chairman shall appoint a Vice-Chairman, who shall not be a full-time employee of the church, and who shall hold office until a new Vice Chairman is appointed. The Vice Chairman shall serve as chairman of the Compensation Task Force during the budget process, and he shall chair Elders' Meetings at the Chairman's discretion.

Section 3.

The Chairman and Vice-Chairman shall retain at all times the right to act on any question, commensurate with every other Elder.

Section 4.

Pursuant to §2.2.4 of the Constitution, the Chairman may appoint a Representative to serve as Moderator of any Members' Meeting. This may be, but is not required to be, the Vice-Chairman.

Section 5.

In his capacity as Secretary, the Senior Pastor may appoint an Assistant, not necessarily an Elder, to keep, compile, and archive the Minutes of the Board. Minutes, including Attendance Records, shall be kept for every Meeting of the Board, except when the Board is in Executive Session. Minutes shall be made available to all Elders within seven days of every meeting.

Section 6.

In the event of a vacancy in the Senior Pastorate, the Elders shall elect an Interim Chairman.

Section 7.

No other Officers of the Board shall be recognized.

ARTICLE 3. MEETINGS

Section 1.

Regular Meetings of the Board shall be scheduled upon the recommendation of the Chairman and the consent of a Majority of the Elders present and voting on the question. The Regular Meetings of the Board shall take place at least once in every month, and additionally for at least five minutes immediately prior to every Members' Meeting. The public announcements of Members' Meetings and the Minutes of the Board, duly delivered according to §2.5 of these By-Laws, shall constitute due Notice of Regular Meetings.

Section 2.

A Special Meeting of the Board shall be called within one week of the application of a Majority of the Full Number of

Elders to the Chairman, or at the Chairman's discretion.

Section 3.

No Meeting of the Board shall be held without Notice of such Meeting being given to every Elder at least two days in advance, except by Unanimous Consent.

Section 4.

Pursuant to §3.2.9 of the Constitution, the Board may not exclude any Elder from any Meeting of the Board, or any portion thereof, without his consent or the concurrence of three-quarters of the Full Number of Elders, except as directed in Article 6 of these By-Laws. Even if an Elder is to be duly excluded by the Board, notice of any meeting must still be given to all Elders, pursuant to §3.3 of these By-Laws.

Section 5.

Visitors may be invited to Meetings of the Board by a Majority Vote of the Elders, or by the Chairman or Vice-Chairman without objection from any other Elder.

Section 6.

During any Meeting, the Board may enter Executive Session, defined as a Private Session of the Board Members, by majority vote of the Elders present and voting on the question, or at the discretion of the Chairman without objection by any other Elder. The Board may exit Executive Session by the same procedure. The Board must enter Executive Session at least once in every Regular Meeting for at least five minutes, those meetings held immediately before Members' Meetings being excepted. All business shall be in order during Executive Session, subject to these By-Laws. The nomination of new Elders may occur only in Executive Session. Minutes shall not be taken of proceedings in Executive Session. By unanimous consent of the Elders present, visitors may be invited to Executive Session.

Section 7.

Upon the request of any Elder to the Chairman, any item of discussion or business shall be referred to Executive Session.

Section 8.

An Elders' Retreat—defined as a meeting lasting at least eighteen consecutive hours, held between September 1 and December 31, and passing through 4am on a Saturday morning—shall be held once every calendar year. A Retreat shall be scheduled by means of a Poll of the Elders, to be completed no later than August 15 of each year and according to the following requirements: Only those dates which can be attended by every Elder elected under §3.3 and §3.4 of the Constitution shall be eligible; after that, the eligible date with the most available Elders shall be the date of the Retreat; in case of a tie, the earliest eligible date engaged in the tie shall be the date of the Retreat. The Retreat shall be held according to the Elders' declared ability to attend during the Poll, not their actual ability to attend. The Retreat shall be considered Executive Session, and the Elders present at the Retreat shall constitute a Quorum, except for questions governed under Article 6 of these By-Laws. The Chairman shall decide the agenda for the Retreat. All business shall be in order during the Retreat, subject to these By-Laws.

ARTICLE 4. EXPECTATIONS

Section 1.

Each Elder shall be expected to be present for at least Two-Thirds of the Meetings of the Board, both Regular and Special, excepting those held immediately prior to Members' Meetings. Failure to do so over a consecutive twelve-month period shall be duly considered by the Board in the matter of Re-nomination, Censure, Request for Resignation, or Recommendation for Removal.

ARTICLE 5. BUDGET PROCESS

Section 1.

Pursuant to the Constitution §4.2.1, the Elders shall present an approved Proposed Budget to the Deacon of Finance at least one week before the penultimate Members' Meeting of each Fiscal Year. In the event of a failure by the Elders to approve a new Proposed Budget in time, the most recent Budget adopted by the Church, with its amendments, shall be presented to the Deacon of Finance as the approved Proposed Budget.

Section 2.

The process of creating and adopting a Proposed Budget, including the definition of a Quorum for Budget Meetings, shall be governed by the "[NAME OF CHURCH] Budget Process," which may be amended by a Majority of the Full Number of Elders.

Section 3.

As part of the budget process, and upon the consent of the Elders present and voting on the question at the meeting prescribed by the [NAME OF CHURCH] Budget Process, the Vice-Chairman shall appoint a Compensation Task Force to be chaired by the Vice Chairman, and to include the Deacon of Finance, no other non-elder, not more than three other elders, no full-time staff elders, and a majority of the entire task force not being in the pay of the church. The Associate Pastor for Administration shall attend meetings and have a voice for informational purposes, but shall not have a vote, and shall be dismissed when his own compensation is discussed. The sole responsibility of the Compensation Task Force shall be to recommend to the Board, with the advice of the Senior Pastor, Compensation packages, defined as Salary plus Housing, for the church's staff, and after its report it shall immediately dissolve.

Section 4.

A Proposed Budget shall be approved and recommended to the Deacon of Finance by a Majority of the Full Number of Elders.

ARTICLE 6. NOMINATION OF NEW ELDERS

Section 1.

These By-Laws shall be subordinate to Article 3 of the Constitution.

Section 2.

The Nomination of a New Elder shall proceed with two Votes by the Full Number of Elders, the first to send the potential Nominee the "Questionnaire for Potential Elders," and the second to Nominate. Votes under this Article shall take place in Executive Session and only when a Quorum of three-quarters of the Full Number of Elders is present. For Votes under §6.5 of these By-Laws, the Elder under consideration shall not be considered in the calculation of the Quorum, nor counted toward its fulfillment.

Section 3.

The Vote to send a potential Nominee the Questionnaire shall proceed as follows: During any Executive Session, and a Quorum being present, an Elder shall Propose the name of a potential Nominee for Elder. After discussion, the Chairman shall ask if any Elder votes Nay; if a Nay is declared by simultaneous show of hands, the proposal fails; if not, then the Chairman shall ask if any Elder Abstains; if Abstentions amounting to one-fifth of the Full Number of Elders are declared by simultaneous show of hands, the proposal fails; if not, the Chairman shall confirm that all other Elders present vote Yea. If the proposal survives, any Elder not present must be notified of the proposal immediately and allowed to cast a vote within twenty-four hours. Elders not present may vote by Correspondence, but any Elder not voting shall be considered to have Abstained. One Nay or Abstentions amounting to one-fifth of the Full Number of Elders shall prevent the sending of the Questionnaire. Otherwise, the Questionnaire shall be sent to the potential nominee.

Section 4.

The Vote to Nominate a New Elder shall proceed as follows: During any Executive Session, and a Quorum being present, an Elder shall Propose the name of a potential Nominee for Elder, provided he has returned the completed Questionnaire and the Elders have had one day to consider it. After discussion, the Chairman shall ask if any Elder votes Nay; if a Nay is declared by simultaneous show of hands, the proposal fails; if not, then the Chairman shall ask if any Elder Abstains; if Abstentions amounting to one-fifth of the Full Number of Elders are declared by simultaneous show of hands, the proposal fails; if not, the Chairman shall confirm that all other Elders present vote Yea. If the proposal survives, any Elder not present must be notified of the proposal immediately and allowed to cast a vote within twenty-four hours. Elders not present may vote by Correspondence, but any Elder not voting shall be considered to have Abstained. One Nay or Abstentions amounting to one-fifth of the Full Number of Elders shall prevent the Nomination. Otherwise, the nominee shall be presented to the church for election pursuant to the Constitution.

Section 5.

Any Elder finishing his term and eligible for re-election pursuant to §3.2.6 of the Constitution shall receive an automatic Vote, timed so as to prevent any gap in his eldership, and governed by §6.4 of these By-Laws, except that he shall not be required to complete the Questionnaire unless otherwise directed by a Majority vote of the Elders present and voting.

Section 6.

No other Person shall receive an automatic Vote, but shall be nominated only upon the completion of the entire Nomination process described in §6.2-4 of these By-Laws.

Section 7.

No Person under consideration for nomination or re-nomination as an Elder shall be present for the Vote process concerning him, and he shall not be privy to the discussions or proceedings therein. An Elder considered under §6.5 of these By-Laws shall be privy only to whether or not he will be renominated and a general description of the reasons for the decision, but the votes of particular Elders shall not be revealed.

Section 8.

Votes taken under Article 6 of these By-Laws shall be considered Final until a) the Elders by Unanimous Consent agree to reconsider a Proposal; or b) a new duly-called Meeting of the Board is called to order.

Section 9.

Both the Votes and the Deliberations of the Board during proceedings under Article 6 of these By-Laws shall be considered Strictly Confidential. Except when explicitly directed by Unanimous Consent of the Board, any Violation of that Confidentiality shall be considered grounds for Censure, a Request for Resignation, or a Recommendation for Removal, pursuant to Article 7 of these By-Laws.

ARTICLE 7. DISCIPLINE

Section 1.

These By-Laws shall be subordinate to §3.2.18 of the Constitution.

Section 2.

The Board may Censure any Elder by Majority Vote of the Full Number of Elders. A second Majority Vote of the Full Number of Elders shall be required to report a Censure to the Church at the next Regular Members' Meeting. Otherwise the Censure shall remain confidential.

Section 3.

The Board may formally Request, but not require, the Resignation of any Elder by Majority Vote of the Full Number of Elders. A second Majority Vote of the Full Number of Elders shall be required to report a Request for Resignation to the Church at the next Regular Members' Meeting. Otherwise the Request for Resignation shall remain confidential.

Section 4.

The Board may formally Recommend to the Church the Removal of an Elder from office by Two-Thirds Vote of the Full Number of Elders.

ARTICLE 8. ADOPTION AND AMENDMENT

Section 1.

These By-Laws shall be adopted upon the approval of a Majority of the Full Number of Elders.

Section 2.

These By-Laws shall be amended upon a Two-Thirds Vote of the Full Number of Elders.

Made in the USA
Columbia, SC
11 October 2022